# ESOL
# Practice Grammar

*Supplementary Grammar Support for ESOL Students*

ENTRY LEVEL 3

David King

*Garnet*
EDUCATION

# Introduction

### Who is it for?

The book is designed primarily, but not exclusively, for adult students studying ESOL at schools and colleges in the United Kingdom.

It can be used to support topic- and function-based class work. Alternatively, students can use it for self-study or for their own reference.

The rationale underlying the book is to make grammar accessible, relevant and memorable. This is done by making use of step-by-step activities and clear contextualized language.

### Level

The material takes the Key Grammatical Structures at Entry Level 3 from the Adult ESOL core curriculum as its basis. It also recycles aspects of the Entry Level 2 curriculum.

We know that the language profile of ESOL students at or around 'pre-intermediate' level is rarely an exact match for the Adult ESOL core curriculum level specifications. The book therefore attempts to take this 'spikey profile' of ESOL classes into account through accessible explanations and graded practice exercises.

### Content

The book contains 26 two-page or four-page units, followed by grammar notes, appendices and an answer key.

### Approach

The approach used in *ESOL Practice Grammar* asks students to infer the pattern or rule from context, rather than making overt statements about the language, to encourage genuine language development.

The 'Use in Context' section in each unit presents the grammar point through a realistic scenario, usually a naturalistic dialogue involving characters that ESOL students can identify with. Students are then asked to focus on key elements of the language to help them understand the pattern or rule. Further clarification is provided by referring the students to appropriate grammar notes at the back of the book.

A set of exercises practising the grammar point follows each 'Use in Context'. These exercises are designed to account for differentiation within a class by offering a progressive degree of challenge. Where appropriate, the final exercise personalizes the grammar point with communicative interaction.

# Contents

1  The present: present simple and continuous

2  The future: present continuous, *going to*, *will*

3  The past: past simple and continuous

4  Past situations and habits: *used to*

5  Present perfect 1: *Have you ever …? How long have you …?*

6  Present perfect 2: an unfinished timeframe

7  Present perfect 3: present perfect or past simple?

8  Sentences with *if* and *when*: zero and first conditionals

9  The verbs *be* and *have*

10  Indirect (embedded) questions

11  Simple reported statements

12  Reported questions

13  Verb forms 1: *~ing*, *to ~* or *to ~*?

14  Verb forms 2: some other uses of *~ing* and *to~* verb forms

15  Modal verbs 1: obligation and advice

16  Modal verbs 2: future possibility and requests

17  Relative pronouns 1: subject pronouns – *who / which / that / whose*

18  Relative pronouns 2: when *who / that / which / where* is not necessary

19  Linking words: *and, also, but, or, so, because, as, although*

20  The definite article: *the*

21  Adjectives 1: comparatives and superlatives

22  Adjectives 2: *less, a lot / a bit, (not) as ~ as, too ~, ~enough*

23  Quantity: *some, any, much, many, a lot (of), a few, a little, all, most*

24  Prepositions of time

25  Prepositions: after adjectives and verbs; prepositional phrases

26  Phrasal verbs

Grammar notes

Answer key

# The present
## present simple and continuous

## Use in context 1: present simple and adverbs of frequency

Nargis is talking to Surinder. Read what they say.
Look at the words in **bold**.

Nargis

Surinder

**Nargis:** So, **do you go** out to work, Surinder?

**Surinder:** Yes, I **work** in an office, but I **don't work** full-time. I only **do** part-time because of my children. **I usually take** them to school in the morning and **pick** them up in the afternoon.

**Nargis:** And what about your husband, what **does he do**?

**Surinder:** He **works** as a driver for a cleaning company. It's hard work, but he **enjoys** his job because he **meets** lots of different people.

**Nargis:** **Does he work** at weekends?

**Surinder:** He **sometimes works** on Saturday mornings. He **doesn't go** to work on Sundays so **we're always** together as a family for at least one day.

We use the present simple to talk about habits, general actions and things that are normally true.

With frequency adverbs, it may help to think about what percentage of the time something is true:

Never = 0%          Usually = 90%
Sometimes = 20–50%   Always = 100%
Often = 60%

💡 **How do we make the present simple tense?** (page 82)

**A** Complete these sentences with words from the conversation.

**Statement:**

1  I <u>work</u> in an office.

2  He _____ as a driver.

**Question:**

3  So, _____ out to work, Surinder?

4  _____ at weekends?

**Negative:**

5  I _____ full-time.

6  He _____ to work on Sundays.

💡 **Where do we put adverbs of frequency (*sometimes*, *always*, etc.)?**

**B** Complete these examples from the conversation.

The adverb between the subject and the verb:

1  _____ them to school in the morning.

The adverb after forms of the verb *be*:

2  … so _____ together as a family for at least one day.

## Practice

**1** Write the correct form for these verbs.

| I go | He <u>goes</u> | g They play | She _____ |
|---|---|---|---|
| a You do | She _____ | h They cost | It _____ |
| b We fly | It _____ | i I have | He _____ |
| c I study | He _____ | j I wash | He _____ |
| d You fix | He _____ | k You pay | She _____ |
| e They watch | She _____ | l You drive | He _____ |
| f We make | It _____ | m We carry | It _____ |

**2**  **Use the correct form of one of the verbs in the box to complete each sentence.**

> produce    not rain    play    not cost    use    ~~not like~~    talk    go

She ___doesn't like___ writing letters.

a  _____ your son _____ football?

b  It _____ much in August.

c  _____ you _____ your computer every day?

d  British people always _____ too fast for me to understand.

e  My country _____ a lot of fruit and vegetables.

f  _____ you often _____ swimming in the summer?

g  Food _____ so much in my country.

**3**  **Put the words in the correct order to make sentences.**

pick up / I / the children / from school / always   ___I always pick up the children from school.___

a  usually / in the evenings / television / watch / they _____

b  the college / see / we / him / at / often _____

c  to work / you / do / drive / usually / ? _____

d  go / we / on / for lunch / out / don't / Sundays / always _____

e  on his way / stops at / sometimes / he / home / the supermarket _____

f  from work / your neighbour / home / what time / get / does / ? _____

g  I / never / when / he / the phone / answers / ring _____

**4**  **Work with a classmate. Ask and answer questions using the ideas in the box and the present simple.**

> have for breakfast    watch TV    start work    leave work    go to college
> go to bed    do your shopping    study English    have a shower    have lunch
> read an English newspaper

For example:

A:  *What do you have for breakfast?*
B:  *I usually have cereal and toast.*

*My country produces a lot of vegetables.*

# Use in context 2: present continuous

Cheng sees Kerim in the street. Read what they say. Look at the words in **bold**.

**Cheng**

**Kerim**

**Cheng:** Hi, Kerim! How are you? What **are you doing**?

**Kerim:** Oh, hi there, Cheng! Good to see you. **I'm doing** some shopping. **I'm looking** for a present for my sister. I never know what to buy her.

**Cheng:** Right. How is she? **Is she** still **working** at the burger bar?

**Kerim:** No, **she isn't working** there right now. She's away. **She's staying** with relatives in Turkey. But **I'm working** there for a few weeks to earn some money before I start at university. How about you?

**Cheng:** Well, **I'm not working** at the moment. **I'm taking** a break for the summer. **I'm enjoying** myself doing nothing for a change!

We use the present continuous to talk about things we are doing now, around the present time, or for changing or temporary situations in our lives.

For more information on the present continuous, see page 82.

## How do we make the present continuous tense? (page 82)

**A** **Complete the sentences with words from the conversation.**

**Statement:**

1  I'm doing _____ some shopping.

2  _____ with relatives in Turkey.

**Question:**

3  What _____?

4  _____ still _____ at the burger bar?

**Negative:**

5  No, _____ there right now.

6  Well, _____ at the moment.

**B** **Circle the four time expressions we often use with the present continuous.**

every day    normally    (now)    still
never    right now    usually
generally    at the moment

## Practice

**1** **Write the ~ing forms of these verbs.**

say    _saying_

a  get    _____
b  meet    _____
c  try    _____
d  die    _____

e  make    _____
f  write    _____
g  sleep    _____
h  arrive    _____
i  shut    _____

j  eat    _____
k  have    _____
l  begin    _____
m  visit    _____
n  happen    _____

**2** **A TV presenter is describing an awards ceremony in Hollywood. Write the verbs in brackets in the present continuous tense.**

"I'm standing (stand) here outside the theatre. The fans a_____ (scream) as the stars arrive. Judi Twinkle b_____ (get) out of her car. She c_____ (wear) a fabulous gold dress. Behind her, another car d_____ (arrive). I can see the actor Tom Flight. He e_____ (sit) in the back with his beautiful wife. I think they f_____ (have) an argument. He g_____ (try) to smile for the cameras, but I think she h_____ (cry) in the back of the car. They i_____ (not get) out. Oh dear, now it j_____ (begin) to rain."

**3** **Look at these mini-dialogues. Write A's sentences or questions using the present continuous and the words given.**

**A:** phone / ring

_The phone's ringing._

**B:** Well, can you answer it for me?

a **A:** sun / shine

 

**B:** OK. Let's go out.

b **A:** it / rain / ?

 

**B:** Yes, it's really heavy at the moment.

c **A:** she / have / shower / ?

 

**B:** No, she's still in bed.

d **A:** you / use / computer / ?

 

**B:** No, it's free if you want to use it.

e **A:** kettle / boil

 

**B:** Can you make the tea, please?

f **A:** you / watch / TV / ?

 

**B:** No, you can turn it off now.

g **A:** radio / not / work

 

**B:** It probably needs a new battery.

**4** **Cheng is having a tutorial with his teacher. Circle the correct tense for each verb.**

Teacher: So, Cheng, what **do you think** / **are you thinking** about your English? **Is it improving** / **Does it improve**?

Cheng: Yes, I think my English **is getting** / **gets** better, but **I'm sometimes getting** / **I sometimes get** depressed about my progress. In fact, there are days when I think my English **is getting** / **gets** worse. For example, this afternoon I'm sure **I'm talking** / **I talk** rubbish.

Teacher: That's not true, Cheng. **We're all feeling** / **We all feel** like that sometimes. What about homework? How many hours **are you generally studying** / **do you generally study** at home during the week?

Cheng: Well, to be honest, **I'm not usually doing** / **I don't usually do** much homework. **I'm not having** / **I don't have** enough time after work. But this week, **I'm studying** / **I study** during my lunch break because my exam is next Saturday. Right now, **I'm trying** / **I try** to improve my listening. **I'm always finding** / **I always find** it difficult to understand English people. What **are you thinking** / **do you think** is the best way to improve my listening?

Teacher: Practice, practice, practice. **I'm believing** / **I believe** it's the only way.

**5** **Work with a classmate. Ask and answer questions using the present simple and present continuous. Use these ideas.**

**Present simple**: your daily routine, your work, your normal week, your normal weekend, what you usually do in your spare time.

**Present continuous**: what you are doing now, what you think your friends and family are doing now, temporary or changing situations in your life.

**For example:**

A: _How do you normally spend your weekends?_
B: _We usually go to the shops on Saturdays and we always spend Sundays with my family._

B: _What do you think your best friend's doing now?_
A: _I think she's probably lying on the beach in the sunshine._

## Use in context 1: present continuous, *going to*, *will*

Read the conversation. Look at the words in **bold**.

Deva

**Deva:** My sister **is having** a party on Saturday. **Are you coming**?

**Rafiq:** Yes, great, **I'll come**. **I'll ask** my boss if I can finish work early.

**Deva:** **I'm meeting** my sister on Friday. **We're going to buy** some new clothes. **I'm going to help** her with the food on Saturday morning, too.

Rafiq

**Rafiq:** **Are your brothers coming** to the party?

**Deva:** They don't know about it yet. **I'll phone** them now.

**A** To talk about the future we can use:

1 the present continuous:
My sister <u>is having</u> a party.

2 *going to*: _____ some new clothes.

3 *will*/*won't*: _____ my boss.

**B** Complete the table.

| To talk about: | We use: |
|---|---|
| our intentions, or what we want to do in the future | *going to* |
| definite future arrangements | _____ |
| future things we decide now | _____ |

For more information on the future, see page 82.

## Practice

**1** Look at Vera's diary and complete the conversation using the present continuous.

| | Day | Evening |
|---|---|---|
| **Mon** | teach at university | book club |
| **Tue** | teach | |
| **Wed** | teach | mark projects |
| **Thu** | teach | drive to Bristol |
| **Fri** | attend conference at Bristol University | |
| **Sat** | | |
| **Sun** | meet parents | |

**Elsa:** Hi, Vera. Are you free this week? ___Are___ you ___doing___ anything on Wednesday?

**Vera:** Sorry, but on Wednesday I ª_____ during the day and I ᵇ_____ projects in the evening.

**Elsa:** OK. ᶜ_____ you ᵈ_____ anything on Thursday evening, then?

**Vera:** Oh, I ᵉ_____ to Bristol after work on Thursday. I ᶠ_____ a conference there on Friday.

**Elsa:** ᵍ_____ you ʰ_____ anything at the weekend?

**Vera:** Well, on Sunday I ⁱ_____ my parents, but I ʲ_____ not ᵏ_____ anything on Saturday. Shall I come over to your place around 8.00?

**Elsa:** Yes, that would be great. See you then.

**2** Good intentions! What are the people going to do? Choose a verb from the box to complete these sentences with *going to*.

> babysit    try    change    ~~look~~    lose    study    fly    buy

Cheng _is going to look_ for a better job.

a   Rafiq _____ Deva a watch for her birthday.

b   Ismail _____ hard for his exam.

c   Hamid _____ his old car.

d   Surinder _____ every evening for her sister.

e   Roman _____ home to Lithuania to see his parents.

f   Jeya _____ ten kilos before the summer.

g   Vera _____ to spend more time with her boyfriend.

**3** Match a sentence on the left with the best response on the right.

a   When shall we meet again?                 1   We'll talk about it tomorrow.

b   You need some fresh air!                   2   I'll give you a ring.

c   What are you doing for lunch?              3   Yes, I think we'll have a break.

d   It's 11.00. Fancy a coffee?               4   I think I'll get a sandwich.

e   When can you give me a decision?          5   I think I'll watch a DVD.

f   I've missed my last train!                6   I'll look it up on the Internet.

g   How can we find out what's on at the cinema?   7   Don't worry, I'll give you a lift home.

h   What are you doing tonight?               8   Yes, I think I'll go out for a walk.

**4** Circle the correct option.

Bye, *I'm going to see* / *I'll see* you tomorrow.

a   When I grow up *I'm being* / *I'm going to be* a racing driver.

b   Tomorrow my diary is full. *I'm having* / *I'll have* lunch with a client and *I'm seeing* / *I'll see* the doctor at 5.30.

c   Where's Ismail?

   I don't know. *I'm trying* / *I'll try* his mobile number.

d   This is what I intend to do. First, *I'm painting* / *I'm going to paint* the kitchen, then the hall.

e   Oh, I must get a birthday card for Ling!

   *I'm going to get* / *I'll go and get* one at lunchtime.

**5** Work with a classmate. Ask and answer questions about:

a   definite fixed arrangements for the next month;
b   intentions for the future.

**For example:**

A: *What are you doing this week?*          B: *What do you intend to do for the summer?*
B: *I'm seeing the dentist at 4.30 on Friday.*   A: *I'm going to get fit.*

## Use in context 2: more uses of *will, won't, going to*

Read the conversation. Look at the words in **bold**.

**Ismail**

**Amir**

**Ismail:** I've got a problem. My car **won't start**. Can I borrow yours? I promise **I'll look after** it.

**Amir:** No! You**'ll have** an accident. Can't you go by bus?

**Ismail:** But it**'s going to rain** in a minute! I'll get wet.

For more information on *will, won't, going to*, see page 83.

**A** **Complete the sentences with *will, won't* or *going to*.**

We use:

1  _won't_ when someone or something refuses to do something:

My car _____ .

2  _____ when we make a promise, or a prediction about the future:

No! You _____ an accident.

3  _____ when we are sure about the future result of a present situation:

But it _____ in a minute.

## Practice

**1** **Match a sentence on the left with the best response on the right.**

a  I've got so much work to do.

b  What's the matter with your iPod?

c  Isn't your little girl hungry?

d  I don't know how to get in touch with Abdul.

e  Can you take me to the hospital tomorrow?

f  You really must try to get fit!

g  Can you work late tonight?

h  Can you keep a secret?

1  Of course. I'll pick you up at 9.30.

2  Yes, you can trust me.

3  I'll come and give you a hand.

4  I don't know. It won't work.

5  OK, I'll give up alcohol … but I won't give up smoking!

6  OK, I'll stay until 7.00.

7  No, she won't eat a thing.

8  I'll give you his number.

**2** **Predictions. What do you think will be the world situation in 50 years' time? Write your ideas about some of the things in the box.**

> the world's population    food    travel    oil    the climate    mobile phones    disease
> war    books    getting married    natural disasters    cars    space travel    computers
> religion    the most powerful countries in the world    Africa    work

The world's population will be about ten billion people.

People won't get married anymore.

_____

_____

_____

**3** Look at each picture and write a sentence about what is going to happen. Use the verbs in the box.

> have   ~~have~~   cross   rain   miss   fall off

She's _going to have_ a baby.

a It _____.

b He _____ the ladder.

c He _____ the bus.

d She _____ a party.

e They _____ the road.

**4** Work with a classmate. Ask and answer questions about:

a predictions for the next 12 months;
b things that your partner has promised or refused to do.

**For example:**

A: *Who do you think will win the World Cup?*
B: *I think Brazil will win.*

B: *Is there anything you really won't do?*
A: *Yes, I won't work on Sundays.*

*What's the matter with your iPod?*

# The past
## past simple and continuous

## Use in context 1: past simple

Jan is talking to Cheng. Read what they say. Look at the words in **bold**.

Jan

Cheng

**Jan:** When **did** you **come** to England, Cheng?

**Cheng:** About six months ago. I **didn't know** anybody when **I first arrived**.

**Jan:** Oh, so what did **you do**?

**Cheng:** Luckily, **I got** a job. **I worked** in a hotel where **I met** other people. Also, **I started** English classes so **I soon began** to make new friends.

🔆 **How do we make the past simple tense?** (page 83)

**A** **Complete the sentences with words from the conversation.**

**Negative:**

1   I _____ anybody when I first arrived.

**Questions:**

2   When _____ you _____ to England, Cheng?

3   Oh, so what _____ you _____?

**B** **Cheng uses these verbs:** *arrived, got, worked, met, started, began.* **Write each verb in the correct column.**

| Regular verbs | Irregular verbs |
|---|---|
| arrived | _____ |
| _____ | _____ |
| _____ | _____ |

🔆 **Do we say the endings of the three regular verbs in the same way?** (page 83)

🔆 **When do we use the past simple tense?**

**C** **Tick (✓) the correct statement.**

☐ 1   We use the past simple for finished, completed actions and times.

☐ 2   We use the past simple for times and actions which are still continuing.

For more irregular verbs, see page 89.

## Practice

**1** **Write the past simple forms of these verbs.**

play    <u>played</u>

a   come    _____

b   eat    _____

c   buy    _____

d   write    _____

e   close    _____

f   break    _____

g   tell    _____

h   study    _____

i   leave    _____

j   pay    _____

k   hear    _____

l   open    _____

m   fly    _____

n   try    _____

o   enjoy    _____

p   catch    _____

q   stop    _____

r   teach    _____

s   wear    _____

**2** Look at the three different ways of saying the ~*ed* verb endings. Write each of the regular verbs from the box in the correct column.

| worked [/t/] | arrived [/d/] | started [/ɪd/] |
|---|---|---|
| cooked | | |
| | | |
| | | |
| | | |

> ~~cooked~~    lived    shouted    played
> watched    walked    hated    loved
> waited    called    helped    needed

**3** Circle the five words or phrases which we often use with the past simple.

> (when?)    yesterday    since    ago    today
> now    this morning    last week    these days    what time?

**4** Correct the verbs in these sentences.

I **go** to the cinema a week ago.  _____went_____

a   She **picks** up her children at 3.30 yesterday.  _____

b   Jaani **comes not** to the party last Saturday.  _____

c   **Does** he **took** the train to Manchester last weekend?  _____

d   **Called you** your family last night?  _____

e   I **don't went** to college last week because we **are having** a half-term holiday.  _____

f   What time **had you** breakfast yesterday?  _____

g   They **bought not** a new car last week because they **not have** enough money.  _____

**5** Complete this conversation with the correct past simple forms of the verbs in brackets.

A: Where ___did___ you ___go___ (*go*) for your holiday last summer?

B: We ᵃ_____ (*go*) to Florida.

A: Oh, nice. ᵇ_____ you ᶜ_____ (*see*) Disneyland?

B: Yes, we ᵈ_____ (*do*). We ᵉ_____ (*have*) a great time there, but we ᶠ_____ (*not stay*)
there all the time. We ᵍ_____ (*have*) two weeks so we ʰ_____ (*hire*) a car and
ⁱ_____ (*travel*) around a bit.

A: ʲ_____ you ᵏ_____ (*get*) to the West Coast?

B: No, we ˡ_____ (*not go*) there. We ᵐ_____ (*see*) most of Florida, but we also
ⁿ_____ (*spend*) some time on the beach. So for the second week we ᵒ_____ (*swim*),
we ᵖ_____ (*eat*) good food and just ۹_____ (*relax*).

# Use in context 2: past continuous

Read Ling's story. Look at the words in **bold**.

Ling

" At six o'clock last night I **was sitting** in the college canteen with my friend Cheng. He **was having** a cup of tea and I **was drinking** a cola. We **were chatting** about the class. While I **was explaining** something, my chair suddenly broke and I fell on the floor. Cheng **was laughing** so much that he dropped his cup of tea! "

## How do we make the past continuous tense? (page 83)

**A** Complete this table with the correct past continuous forms.

| Subject | Auxiliary | Negative | Verb | |
|---------|-----------|----------|------|---|
| I | _____ | | _laughing_ _____ | (laugh) |
| You | were | | _____ | (drink) |
| He/She/It | _____ | not (n't) | _____ | (have) |
| We | _____ | | _____ | (chat) |
| They | were | | _____ | (sit) |

## When do we use the past continuous tense? Look at these example sentences from Ling's story. (page 83)

1 At six o'clock last night I was sitting in the college canteen with my friend Cheng.

2 He was having a cup of tea and I was drinking a cola.

3 We were chatting about the class.

4 While I was explaining something, my chair suddenly broke and I fell on the floor.

**B** Now write the number of the example sentence next to the best description of its use.

We use the past continuous to:

a [3] say what was happening over a period of time in the past.

b ☐ describe a past action or situation which was unfinished when it was interrupted by another action.

c ☐ talk about an action or situation happening at an exact time in the past.

d ☐ describe two actions which were happening at the same time in the past.

## Practice

**1** Correct the mistake in each sentence.

We were ~~driveing~~ to work at 8.15 this morning.          _driving_

a Were you writting to your parents when I came in?          _____

b He didn't listening while you were talking.          _____

c Did you were having a meeting when I phoned?          _____

d She were still working at 7 o'clock last night.          _____

e You was wearing a lovely dress last night.          _____

f It wasn't rain during the night.          _____

g He wasn't knowing my name.          _____

**2** Work with a classmate. Ask and answer questions using the past continuous tense.

**For example:**

A: *What were you doing at …?* (e.g., *8.30 Sunday morning/this time yesterday*)
*What were you doing when …?* (e.g., *the class started/the fire alarm rang*)
*What were you doing while …?* (e.g., *the teacher was writing on the board*)

## 3 Circle the correct option: past simple or past continuous.

We *had* / *were having* a meeting when the fire alarm *started* / *was starting* to ring.

a I *still slept* / *was still sleeping* at 11.30 yesterday morning when the postman *came* / *was coming*.

b It *rained* / *was raining* hard all the time while I *drove* / *was driving* on the motorway.

c I *came* / *was coming* to England in January.

d I *hated* / *was hating* my time at secondary school.

e When I *came* / *was coming* back from holiday, our plane *had* / *was having* to make an emergency landing.

f The children were very quiet last night. John was *reading* / *read* while Pat *was watching* / *watched* TV.

## 4 Choose the best verb from the box to complete this story.

| | | | | | |
|---|---|---|---|---|---|
| ordered | played | were drinking | was playing | stopped | began |
| was raining | were playing | decided | stood | were walking | |
| came | went | ~~were having~~ | returned | started | |

While we were having breakfast on Saturday, we a__________ to play tennis. While we b__________ to the tennis courts, it c__________ to rain. We d__________ under a tree while it e__________. When the rain f__________, we g__________ tennis. We h__________ tennis when the rain i__________ again. So, we j__________ into a café and we k__________ a cup of tea. While we l__________ our tea, the sun m__________ out. When we n__________ to our court, someone else o__________ there.

## 5 Complete this story with the correct form of the verbs in brackets.

Last Tuesday I decided (*decide*) to work late. At about 7.30, I a__________ (*wait*) at the bus stop to go home. It b__________ (*rain*) hard.

While I c__________ (*stand*) there, I d__________ (*see*) an old man coming along the street with his dog. The old man e__________ (*stop*) and f__________ (*ask*) me the time. He g__________ (*realise*) I wasn't English and asked me where I h__________ (*come*) from and what I i__________ (*do*) in England.

While we j__________ (*chat*), the bus k__________ (*go*) past without stopping. The old man l__________ (*stop*) chatting and m__________ (*continue*) on his walk.

It was now 7.45 and I n__________ (*feel*) wet and angry, so I o__________ (*start*) to walk home. When I p__________ (*get*) home, I q__________ (*turn*) on the evening news and r__________ (*hear*) about a terrible bus accident. Yes, it was the same bus that had gone past me at the bus stop!

# 4 Past situations and habits
## used to

## Use in context

Ling is talking to Jeya. Read what they say. Look at the words in **bold**.

Ling

Jeya

**Ling:** Is life in England very different from your life in Sri Lanka?

**Jeya:** Yes, it's very different.

**Ling: Did you use to live** with your parents in Sri Lanka?

**Jeya:** Yes, I **did**. I **used** to help my mother cook and look after the home.

**Ling: Did** you **use to** go out to work?

**Jeya:** No, I **didn't**. I **didn't use to** work but now I work in the supermarket and look after my family as well!

☀ **How do we use *used to*?** (page 83)

**A** **Complete these sentences with words from the conversation.**

**Statement:**

1  In Sri Lanka, I <u>used</u> to help my mother.

**Question:**

2  _____ you _____ go out to work?

**Short answers:**

3  Yes, I _____ . /No, I _____ .

**Negative:**

4  I _____ work, but now I work in the supermarket.

☀ **When do we use *used to*?**

**B** **Only one of these sentences is correct. Tick (✓) the correct sentence.**

1  ☐ We use *used to* for present habits and situations.

2  ☐ We use *used to* for past habits and situations which were true but are not true now.

☀ **Used to or *usually*?**

**Read what Jeya says.**
*The climate's much colder here. When I lived in Sri Lanka **I used to wear** summer clothes all the time, but here in England **I usually wear jeans**, a sweater and a coat.*

**C** **Circle the correct option, *used to* or *usually*.**

1  We use **used to** / (usually) for present habits and situations.

2  We use **used to** / **usually** for past habits and situations.

## Practice

**1** **Correct the mistake in each sentence.**

I used to ~~played~~ basketball when I was younger.      _____play_____

a  She was used to have long hair.      _____

b  Did you used to live in London?      _____

c  There used to being more shops in our High Street.      _____

d  I don't use to work hard at school.      _____

e  My parents didn't used to talk to each other.      _____

f  When I was small I use to love ice-cream.      _____

g  I used to have a big party on my 18th birthday.      _____

**2** Ling is asking Jeya some more questions about her life in Sri Lanka. Complete the conversation with the correct form of *used to*.

Ling: _Did you use to_ live in a city in Sri Lanka?

Jeya: No, I ᵃ_____. We ᵇ_____ live in a small village. All my family, my cousins, uncles, aunts and grandparents ᶜ_____ live together.

Ling: So, ᵈ_____ see a lot of your family?

Jeya: Yes, I ᵉ_____. We ᶠ_____ see each other all the time. I really miss them now. Of course, sometimes we ᵍ_____ argue, but I ʰ_____ feel lonely. There always ⁱ_____ be someone to talk to. We ʲ_____ have such a happy time!

**3** Past and present habits. Complete the sentences with *used to* or *usually*.

In my country I _used to_ drink coffee, but here I _usually_ drink tea.

a   When I was young I _____ play football, but now I _____ just watch it on TV.

b   These days she _____ has a salad, but she _____ eat a hamburger and chips.

c   I _____ enjoy driving, but nowadays I _____ travel by train.

d   I _____ smoke a lot, but now I _____ just have a cigarette on special occasions.

e   Here in England I _____ go out at the weekends, but when I was in my country I _____ go out every evening.

f   In my old job I _____ travel a lot, but in my new job I _____ stay in the office.

**4** Seventy years ago, life in this country was very different from life today. Make sentences with *used to* or *didn't use to*. Choose one verb from the box for each sentence.

> ~~watch~~   have   travel   ride   go   drink   wear

People _didn't use to watch_ television.

a   Most women _____ out to work.

b   People _____ mobile phones.

c   Everybody _____ hats.

d   Very few people _____ abroad for their holidays.

e   People _____ bicycles more than they do now.

f   Children _____ as much cola as they do these days.

**5** Write sentences about yourself with *used to* and the ideas in the box.

**6** Work with a classmate. Ask and answer questions.

For example:

A: *What kind of hairstyle did you use to have?*
B: *I used to have short, straight hair with a fringe at the front.*

> a hairstyle you used to have
> clothes you used to wear
> sports you used to do
> a place you used to live
> things you used to do
> music you used to like

## Use in context

Read the conversation. Look at the words in **bold**.

Ling

Hamid

**Ling:** How long **have** you **lived** in Crawley?

**Hamid:** For nearly six months. Before that I lived in Islamabad.

**Ling:** In Pakistan?

**Hamid:** Yes. It's the capital. **Have** you ever **been** to Pakistan?

**Ling:** No, I **haven't**.

💡 **How do we make the present perfect simple tense?** (page 83)

**A** Complete this table with the correct present perfect simple forms.

| Subject | Auxiliary | Negative | Past participle | |
|---|---|---|---|---|
| I | _____ | | *been* | (be) |
| You | _____ | | _____ | (live) |
| He/She/It | _____ | (not) n't | _____ | (phone) |
| We | *have* | | _____ | (ring) |
| They | *have* | | | |

**B** Complete these questions with words from the conversation.

1  <u>Have</u> you ever <u>been</u> to Pakistan?

2  How long _____ you _____ in Crawley?

💡 **When do we use the present perfect simple?**

**C** Here are two sentences using the present perfect. Write the number of the sentence next to the rule that describes it.

1  Have you ever been to Pakistan?

2  How long have you lived in Crawley?

We use the present perfect simple tense to talk about:

a  ☐ something which started in the past and is continuing now. (*How long ...?*)

b  ☐ past experiences at some time in our lives. (*... ever ...?*)

For more information on the present perfect, see page 83.

## Practice

**1** Write the past participles (3rd forms) of these verbs.

do    <u>done</u>

a  buy    _____
b  get    _____
c  grow    _____
d  have    _____
e  leave    _____
f  lose    _____

g  see    _____
h  be    _____
i  go    _____
j  meet    _____
k  think    _____
l  write    _____
m  choose    _____

n  put    _____
o  ride    _____
p  agree    _____
q  travel    _____
r  drive    _____
s  try    _____

**2** Circle the correct verb forms in these sentences.

They *has* / *have* *living* / *lived* in the same house for 20 years.

a   *Have* / *Were* you ever *going* / *been* to India?

b   She *hasn't* / *haven't seen* / *saw* the new movie.

c   *Have* / *Were* you ever *study* / *studied* English before?

d   We *have* / *did* never *fly* / *flown* in a helicopter.

e   I *has* / *have visit* / *visited* a lot of different countries.

f   *Does* / *Has* he *had* / *have* his car long?

**3** Write questions with *ever* using these words. Write a short answer for each question.

you / ever / be / Scotland / ? (Yes)   Have you ever been to Scotland?  Yes, I have.

you / ever / be / Egypt / ? (No)   Have you ever been to Egypt?  No, I haven't.

a   you / ever / try / Indian food / ? (No) _____

b   you / ever / study / English / before / ? (Yes) _____

c   he / ever / send / e-mail / before / ? (No) _____

d   she / ever / drive / in Britain / ? (Yes) _____

e   she / ever / ride / camel / ? (Yes) _____

f   he / ever / speak / you / before / ? (No) _____

**4** Make questions about Vera and Youssef with *How long …?*

Vera's a teacher.   How long has she been a teacher?

a   She lives in London.  How long _____?

b   She teaches at the university.  _____

c   She has a cat.  _____

d   Youssef's a student.  How long _____?

e   He studies music.  _____

f   He plays the piano.  _____

**5** Work with a classmate. Use the ideas in the boxes to ask and answer questions.
Use *Have you ever …?*, *How long have you …?*

For example:

**A:** *Have you ever been to Egypt?*     **B:** *Yes, I have. I went there two years ago.*

**Have you ever …?**

> go / Egypt     try / Indian food     drive / Britain     ride / camel     phone / police
> forget / important date     be / hospital     meet / famous person     be / on TV

**How long have you …?**

> study / English     live / Britain     have / watch     live / present home     be able / swim
> know / best friend     have / present job     have / mobile phone

# Present perfect 2
## an unfinished timeframe

## Use in context

Read the conversation. Look at the words in **bold**.

Teacher

Ismail

**Teacher:** You look different, Ismail. **Have you shaved your moustache?**

**Ismail:** Yes, I shaved it yesterday.

**Teacher:** The class is very small this evening. **Have you seen** Rafiq or Hamid **today?**

**Ismail:** Oh no, **I haven't**, but Hamid texted me. **He's just finished work,** so he'll be a bit late. **Rafiq's gone to London today.** He's taking Deva to Harrods.

**Teacher:** That's nice. **Have you been there yet?**

**Ismail:** Yes, **I've already been to Harrods,** but it's very expensive.

💡 **When do we use the present perfect simple tense?** (page 84)

**A** Here are four example sentences using the present perfect simple. Write the number of the sentence next to the rule that best describes its use.

1 Have you shaved your moustache?

2 Have you been there yet?

3 He's just finished work, so he'll be a bit late.

4 Rafiq's gone to London today.

We use the present perfect simple tense to talk about:

a ☐ things which have *just* happened.

b ☐ recent past events in a time which is still continuing (e.g., today).

c ☐ past actions with present results which we can see.

d ☐ things we have *already* done or we haven't done *yet*.

## Practice

**1** **It's three o'clock. Look at Jeya's list. Has she done all her jobs yet? Make sentences using** *just*, *already* **and** *not ... yet*.

phone dentist ✓ (2.55)

pick up kids at 3.30

do shopping ✓

wash up ✓ (2.50)

peel potatoes ✓

cook evening meal

make beds ✓

do English homework

She ___has just phoned___ the dentist.

a She _____ up the kids _____.

b She _____ the shopping.

c She _____ up.

d She _____ the potatoes.

e She _____ the evening meal _____.

f She _____ the beds.

g She _____ her English homework _____.

**2** **A teacher and her students are talking together in class. Match a sentence on the left with the correct response on the right.**

a   I don't understand this at all!

b   Whose homework is this?

c   I've forgotten my book.

d   What's that noise?

e   It's too cold in here!

f   Do you need to borrow a pen?

g   I've got a different answer to everyone else.

1   Someone's forgotten to turn off their mobile!

2   Well, you'll have to share with a neighbour.

3   Yes, please. Mine's run out of ink.

4   Sorry, I've forgotten to put my name on it.

5   That's because you've done the wrong exercise!

6   Someone's opened all the windows!

7   That's because you've missed too many lessons!

**3** **Rafiq came to England three years ago. A lot of things in his life have changed since then. Complete each sentence about Rafiq using the present perfect form of a verb from the box.**

> start    get    change    ~~learn~~    save    grow    move    buy

He _____ *has learnt* _____ to drive.

a   He _____ to Crawley.

b   He _____ his job.

c   He _____ married.

d   He _____ enough money to buy a car.

e   He _____ a flat.

f   He _____ a moustache.

g   He _____ studying English at college.

**4** **Work with a classmate. Ask and answer questions. Use the present perfect.**

**For example:**

A:  *What have you done today?*
B:  *I've done the shopping and I've cleaned the house.*

A:  *Have you been to London yet?*
B:  *No, I haven't.*

A:  *How has your life changed since you came here?*
B:  *I've started learning English.*

*She has just picked up the kids.*

# Present perfect 3
## present perfect or past simple?

## Use in context

Read the conversation. Look at the words in **bold**.

**Surinder**

**Rafiq**

**Surinder: Have you ever been** to Scotland?

**Rafiq:** Yes, **I have**.

**Surinder: When did you go?**

**Rafiq:** I **was** there last summer. I **went** to Edinburgh. That was after I left London and before I came to Crawley.

**Surinder: How long did you live** in London?

**Rafiq:** For about 18 months before I moved to Crawley.

**Surinder:** And **how long have you been** a taxi driver?

**Rafiq:** For about six months now.

**Surinder:** I see **you've bought** a new taxi.

**Rafiq:** Yes, I'm really pleased with it.

💡 **When do we use the past simple or present perfect?** (page 84)

**A** **Look at the conversation and write *past simple* or *present perfect*.**

1 at some time in your life (*ever*)

   *present perfect*

2 questions with *When*

   _____

3 finished, past times (*last summer*)

   _____

4 finished situations (*before I moved to Crawley*) _____

5 continuing situations (*for about six months now*) _____

6 situations where you can see a present change _____

## Practice

**1** **We often use six of these words and phrases with the past simple and six with the present perfect. Write them in the correct column.**

> ~~When?~~   this week   last Tuesday   yet   just   What time?
> since   yesterday   ago   already   ever   last week

| Past simple | Present perfect |
|---|---|
| When? | |
| | |
| | |
| | |
| | |
| | |

**2** **Complete the sentences with a verb from the box, using the present perfect or past simple.**

> see   visit   do   have   do   go   begin   lose
> do   prepare   ~~miss~~   wash up   go   start

Oh dear! I _'ve_____ just __missed__ my train!

1 **A:** _____ you ever _____ Shanghai?

 **B:** Yes, I _____ there last year.

2 **A:** When _____ you _____ doing karate?

 **B:** I _____ having lessons a year ago.

3 **A:** What's the matter with Ling?

 **B:** She _____ her contact lens.

4 Ismail _____ already _____ the meal, but he _____n't _____ yet.

5 **A:** _____ you _____ that programme about Somalia on the TV last night?

 **B:** No, I _____n't.

6 Vera _____ her present cat for five years.

7 **A:** _____ you _____ your homework?

 **B:** Yes, I _____ it before I _____ to work this morning.

**3** **Circle the correct option to complete this story about Hamid.**

Hamid *has just come* / *just came* back from Pakistan. He ᵃ*has been* / *went* there for a three-week holiday. When he ᵇ*has been* / *was* in Pakistan, he ᶜ*has visited* / *visited* all his relatives and he ᵈ*had* / *has had* a really great time.

He ᵉ*has been* / *went* home to Pakistan three times ᶠ*since* / *for* he first ᵍ*has come* / *came* to live in England two years ʰ*since* / *ago*.

He ⁱ*has only arrived* / *only arrived* back in England last weekend, but he ʲ*has already phoned* / *already phoned* Rafiq to tell him about his holiday. However, he ᵏ*hasn't unpacked* / *didn't unpack* and he ˡ*hasn't done* / *didn't do* all his washing ᵐ*yet* / *ago*.

**4** **Work with a classmate. Ask and answer questions about Hamid. Use the present perfect or past simple.**

Where / he / be / ?

**A:** *Where has he been?*
**B:** *He's been to Pakistan.*

a   How long / he / stay / Pakistan / ?

b   What / he / do / Pakistan / ?

c   How many times / he / be / Pakistan / ?

d   When / he / come / live / England / ?

e   When / he / arrive back / ?

f   What / he / do / since / he / come back / ?

g   What / he not / do / yet / ?

*Where's he been?*

# Sentences with *if* and *when*
## zero and first conditionals

## Use in context

Ling wants to open a bank account. Cheng is giving her some advice. Look at the words in **bold**.

Ling

Cheng

**Ling:** How do I get a bank account?

**Cheng:** **If** you **go** to the bank, you **can ask** for advice. **Take** your passport with you **if** you **want** to open an account. Oh, **if** you **open** a savings account, you **get** more interest.

**Ling:** Thanks, maybe I'll go to the bank this afternoon.

**Cheng:** OK, **if** you **go** to the bank, **I'll come** with you.

**Ling:** OK. **I'll let** you know **when** I **go**.

**A** **Complete these sentences with words from the conversation.**

1 _____ you _____ a savings account, you _____ more interest.

2 _____ you _____ to the bank, you _____ _____ for advice.

3 _____ your passport with you _____ you _____ to open an account.

4 _____ you _____ to the bank, I' _____ _____ with you.

5 OK. _____ you know _____ I _____ .

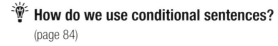 **How do we make conditional sentences?**
(page 84)

**B** **Look at the conversation and write *T* (true) or *F* (false) after these rules.**

1 We use *if* in conditional sentences. T
2 Conditional sentences have two parts.
3 We sometimes use a comma between the two parts of the sentence.
4 We always use *if* at the beginning of a sentence.
5 Sometimes we can use *when* or *if*.

**How do we use conditional sentences?**
(page 84)

**Zero (0) conditional sentences:**

• tell us about a fact, something that is always true.

• use *if* + present tense …, present tense.

**First (1st) conditional sentences:**

• tell us about something that will **possibly** happen.

• use *if* + present tense first clause + future/modal/imperative second clause.

**C** **Which sentence is a zero conditional?**

1 If you open a savings account, you get more interest.
2 If you go to the bank, I'll come with you.

## Practice

**1** **Correct the mistake in each of these first conditional sentences.**

If the sun ~~will shine~~, we can go swimming. ___shines___

a I'll tell him your news when I'll see him. _____

b If there'll be a lot of students, we'll need a bigger room. _____

c If it won't rain soon, my flowers will die. _____

d Do you marry him if he asks you? _____

e  We'll miss the train if we won't hurry up. _____

f  If she hasn't got any money, she doesn't go out this evening. _____

**2  Vera is showing a student how to use the photocopier. She uses zero conditionals. Match the first half of the sentence on the left with the correct ending on the right.**

a  The machine turns on when

b  Open the top if

c  Select the number of copies if

d  Press the green switch when

e  Cancel the copying if

f  Turn off the machine when

1  you want to make copies from a book.

2  you have more than one copy to make.

3  you finish.

4  there is a problem.

5  you are ready to start copying.

6  you press the on/off switch.

**3  Circle the correct option: *when* or *if*.**

I'm not expecting any calls, but *when* / (*if*) the phone rings say I'm out.

a  I'll take a holiday *when* / *if* the spring comes.

b  *When* / *If* you first arrive in this country, you must register with the police.

c  You'll fail your exam *when* / *if* you don't work harder.

d  Cheng only has four more weeks in his job. He'll be very pleased *when* / *if* he leaves.

e  *When* / *If* he wakes up, he always has a shower.

f  Is it OK *when* / *if* I use your pen?

**4  Complete these sentences with the correct form of the verbs in brackets.**

1  **Zero conditionals:** If you ___heat___ chocolate, it ___melts___. (*heat, melt*)

a  You _____ weight when you _____ less. (*lose, eat*)

b  If it _____ too cold, you _____ to turn on the heating. (*be, need*)

c  When you _____ a club, you _____ new people. (*join, meet*)

2  **First conditionals:** If the taxi _'s___ late, we_'ll miss__ our train. (*be, miss*)

a  If it _____, the children _____ a snowman. (*snow, build*)

b  Life _____ easier when I _____ to drive. (*be, learn*)

c  Your cold _____ better if you _____ after yourself. (*not get, not look*)

**5  Work with a classmate. Ask and answer questions. Use these ideas.**

**For example:**

A:  *What will you do if you go out this weekend?*
B:  *If I go out this weekend, I'll probably go to a club.*

> If I stay in tonight …    If I pass my exams …    If I get a new job …
> If I stay in this country …    When I next go back to my country …    When I'm older …

# The verbs *be* and *have*

## Use in context 1: *be* as a main verb

Read the conversation. Look at the words in **bold**.

Roman

Surinder

**Roman:** Where **are** you from?

**Surinder:** I**'m** from India.

**Roman:** Oh, and how old **are you**?

**Surinder:** I**'m** 35. And you?

**Roman:** I**'m** 23. How long **have** you **been** here?

**Surinder:** I**'ve been** here for a year. What about you? Why **weren't** you here at the beginning of the term?

**Roman:** I **was** in London.

**Surinder:** **Will** you **be** here for the exam next week?

**Roman:** Yes, I**'ll be** here. **Are** there classes as usual?

**Surinder:** Yes, there**'s** a class on Monday.

💡 **How do we use the verb *be*?** (page 84)

**A** **Complete these sentences with words from the conversation.**

**Present tense:**

1 Where _____ you from?

 I'_____ from India.

2 _____ there classes as usual?

 Yes, there'_____ a class on Monday.

**Past tense:**

3 Why _____ you here at the beginning of the term?

 I _____ in London.

**Present perfect tense:**

4 How long _____ you _____ here?

 I'_____ here for a year.

**Future tense:**

5 _____ you _____ here for the exam next week?

 Yes, I'_____ here.

## Practice

**1** **Circle the correct option.**

She *was* / *were* afraid of the dark when she *was* / *were* a child.

a The boss thinks you *is* / *are* a very good worker.

b I *am* / *have been* in this country since the beginning of last year.

c My children told me that they *wasn't* / *weren't* very happy at school.

d The man on the TV says the weather *is* / *will be* fine tomorrow.

e *Were you* / *Did you were* cold in bed last night?

f My sister *hasn't been* / *haven't been* very well lately.

g She *will be* / *will have* 18 years old tomorrow.

h I*'m not* / *amn't* interested in football.

**2** **Correct the mistake in these sentences.**

Where do you from?                    _Where are you from?_

a   She has 33 years old.            _____

b   He doesn't be very good at English.   _____

c   We was happy to see our friends.     _____

d   I'm will at the station at 8.30.      _____

e   There is very cold today.            _____

f   Did you was at work yesterday?       _____

g   He have been to many countries.      _____

h   What time has it?                    _____

**3** **Complete these sentences with the correct form of *be*.**

_Aren't_____ you cold without a coat?

a   He _____ 25 on his next birthday.

b   There _____ lots of people at the party last Saturday.

c   Where _____ he yesterday morning?

d   No, she _____ interested in football.

e   Do you think the weather _____ fine tomorrow?

f   We _____ in this house since the summer.

g   _____ she _____ at the meeting next week?

h   No, he _____ to visit his mother in hospital yet.

**4** **Work with a classmate. Ask and answer questions with different forms of *be*. Use these ideas.**

> How old are/is …?    Where was/were …?    How long have/has … been in …?
> What is/are there in …?    Where will … be …?    What is/are … interested in?

**For example:**

A: *What is there in your bedroom?*
B: *There's a lot of different furniture.*

B: *How long have you been in Britain?*
A: *I've been here for about two years.*

*No, she isn't interested in football.*

# Use in context 2: *have* as a main verb

Read the conversation. Look at the words in **bold**.

Surinder

Amir

**Surinder:** **Did** you **have** a good time at the party?

**Amir:** No, I **didn't**. I didn't feel well.

**Surinder:** What's the matter?

**Amir:** I**'ve got** a cold.

**Surinder:** Well, **have** you **had** any paracetamol?

**Amir:** No, I **haven't**. I**'ll have** a look to see if I**'ve got** some.

**Surinder:** And you should eat plenty of fruit. **Do** you **have** any oranges?

**Amir:** No, I **don't have** any food at home. I **haven't had** any breakfast.

**Surinder:** Well, you must buy some food. You must eat breakfast if you aren't well!

## How do we use the verb *have*? (page 85)

**A** Complete these sentences with words from the conversation.

**Note:** We often use *have got* to talk about possession and illness (but not a routine or an activity).

**We can say:**

1 I have a cold. *or* I'_____ a cold.

2 Have you got any oranges? *or* _____ you _____ any oranges?

**Past tense:**

3 _____ you _____ a good time at the party?

4 No, I _____.

**Present perfect:**

5 Well, _____ you _____ any paracetamol?

6 No, I _____.

**Future tense:**

7 I'_____ a look to see if I've got some.

## Practice

**1** **Correct the mistake in each of these sentences.**

She ~~do have~~ a job in a good hotel.                    _____has_____

a  Every day after he gets out of bed, Cheng has got a shower.  _____

b  **A:** Did you have a good holiday?

   **B:** Yes, I had.                                     _____

c  **A:** Have you had any problems here in England?

   **B:** No, I hadn't.                                   _____  _____

d  They had have a new car.                              _____

e  We had got a good flight home after our holiday.      _____

f  I had not coffee for breakfast yesterday.             _____

g  Have you get a new mobile phone?                      _____

h  Did you got any change for the parking meter?         _____

**2 Complete these sentences with the correct form of *have* or *have got*.**

I _'ve got_ a headache and I feel terrible.

a **A:** _____ you _____ any children?

 **B:** No, I _____ .

b **A:** There's no food in the fridge.

 **B:** Sorry, I _____ time to go shopping today.

c **A:** _____ you _____ a nice meal last night?

 **B:** Yes, we _____ .

d I usually _____ a sandwich for lunch.

e **A:** Are you OK? _____ you _____ a stomachache?

 **B:** No, I _____ .

f I _____ a job at the moment, but I'm looking for one.

g **A:** You're wet! _____ you just _____ a swim?

 **B:** Yes, we _____ .

h I think I _____ a cheese sandwich for lunch later today.

**3 Work with a classmate. Ask and answer questions with *have* or *have got*. Use these ideas.**

> **Possessions:** family    a car    a house    a computer    a mobile phone
> **Illness:** a cold    a cough    a temperature    a stomachache    a pain
> **Routines:** a shower    breakfast    lunch    dinner    a drink    a cup of tea
> **Activities:** a walk    a holiday    a good time    a party    a meal    an accident

**For example:**

**A:** *Have you got any family?*
**B:** *Yes, I've got two brothers and a sister.*

**B:** *Do you have a shower in the morning?*
**A:** *Yes, I always have a shower after I get up.*

**A:** *Did you have a walk yesterday?*
**B:** *Yes, I had a walk in the park during my lunchtime.*

*You're wet. Have you just had a swim?*

## Use in context

Jan is phoning the college with some questions about his course. Read his questions.

Jan

a Could you tell me how much the course costs?

b Can you tell me when the lessons start?

c Do you know where I need to go?

Jan uses indirect questions because they are more polite or more formal than direct questions. Notice the word order in indirect questions: *Do you know **where I need** to go?* (page 85)

**A** Write the correct questions in the table.

| Direct questions | Indirect (embedded) questions |
|---|---|
| 1 When do _the lessons start_____? | b Can you tell me _____? |
| 2 How much _____? | a Could you tell me _____? |
| 3 Where do _____? | c Do you know _____? |

Look at some more of Jan's questions.

Could you tell me **if** there's a class on Wednesday afternoons?
Do you know **whether** I need to buy any books?

**B** Complete the table with the direct questions.

| Direct questions | Indirect (embedded) questions |
|---|---|
| 1 Is there _____? | Could you tell me if there's a class on Wednesday afternoons? |
| 2 _____? | Do you know whether I need to buy any books? |

## Practice

**1** Put the words in the correct order to make indirect questions.

is / could you tell me / the post office / where / ?    <u>Could you tell me where the post office is?</u>

a she / where / do / lives / you know / ?    _____

b from / the train / leaves / which platform / can you tell me / ?

_____

c costs / how much / I'd like to know / this sweater / ._____

d the paper / have you / is / any idea / where / ?    _____

e I get / please could / the bus station / how / tell me / to / you / ?

_____

f tonight / going / decided / what / to wear / you are / have you / ?

_____

## 2 Correct the mistake(s) in each of these sentences.

Do you know when ~~does~~ the film ~~start~~?          *when the film starts*

a   Can you tell me how much does cost a return ticket?   _____

b   Do you know what did the teacher give us for homework?   _____

c   Do you know from where does come the new student?   _____

d   Have you any idea on which street does she live?   _____

e   Could you tell me which languages have you studied?   _____

f   Have you decided to where are you going on holiday?   _____

## 3 Rewrite these direct questions as indirect ones. Use *Could you tell me*, *Do you know*, etc.

When does the train to London leave?   *Could you tell me when the train to London leaves?*

a   Why isn't the photocopier working?   _____

b   How much milk do you like in your coffee?   _____

c   Where's the nearest toilet?   _____

d   How much does it cost by taxi?   _____

e   What are you going to eat?   _____

f   What's the time?   _____

g   How does this machine work?   _____

## 4 Tick (✓) the correct indirect question for each of these direct questions.

Do you live in
Birmingham?
☐ 1 Can you tell me if you live in Birmingham? ✓
☐ 2 Can you tell me do you live in Birmingham?
☐ 3 Can you tell me where you do live in Birmingham?

a   Is the train
on time?
☐ 1 Could you tell me is the train on time?
☐ 2 Could you tell me does the train come on time?
☐ 3 Could you tell me if the train's on time?

b   Does this bus go
to the hospital?
☐ 1 Do you know does this bus go to the hospital?
☐ 2 Do you know whether this bus goes to the hospital?
☐ 3 Do you know where this bus does go to the hospital?

c   Are you coming
to the college
Open Day?
☐ 1 Please let me know if do you come to the college Open Day.
☐ 2 Please let me know are you coming to the college Open Day.
☐ 3 Please let me know whether you are coming to the college Open Day.

## 5 Change the direct questions into correct indirect questions with *if* or *whether*.

Is this the right platform for London? *Can you tell me if this is the right platform for London?*

a   Do you like fish? Could you tell me whether _____

b   Did anyone phone me yesterday? Do you know _____

c   Are you from Pakistan? Could _____

d   Has the post come? Do _____

e   Is the sports centre open on Sunday evenings? _____

f   Do I have to wear a suit? _____

# Simple reported statements

## Use in context 1: *say* or *tell*?

It's Tuesday evening. The college phones Rafiq. His wife, Deva, answers the phone. Read the conversations. Look at the words in **bold**.

**Secretary**

**Deva**

**Secretary:** Oh, hello, this is the college. I'm afraid the heating's broken down, so there isn't a class for Rafiq this evening. We can't give him a class this week, so there'll be an extra class for him next week.

**Deva:** OK, **I'll tell** him. Thanks for ringing. Bye.

**Secretary:** Bye.

When Rafiq comes in, Deva gives him the message.

**Deva:** The lady from the college rang.

**Rafiq:** Oh? What **did she say to you**?

**Deva:** **She told me** the heating's broken down and **she said** that there isn't a class this evening. **She told me** they can't give you a class this week. **She said** there'll be an extra class next week.

💡 **What is the difference between *say* and *tell*?** (page 85)

**A** Write *say* or *tell* in the sentences to complete the rule.

1  We normally _____ someone something.

2  We normally _____ something (**to** someone).

## Practice

**1** Circle the correct option: *say* or *tell*.

He *said* / (*told*) me he's going home.

a  She *said* / *told* she's washing her hair.

b  Why didn't you *say* / *tell* the teacher you can't understand the lessons?

c  She *said* / *told* that she likes films.

d  She never *says* / *tells* him what she does.

e  The police *said* / *told* they think the burglar will rob again.

f  Did you *say* / *tell* the doctor what's wrong with you?

g  Did I *say* / *tell* who I saw last night?

h  I'm *saying* / *telling* you the truth.

i  I *said* / *told* to my boss what I really think.

**2** **Complete the sentences with the correct word from the box.**

> I   me   my   you   he   him   ~~her~~   her   they

a   "I love you."

He told _her_ that _____ loves _____.

b   "We're going out now."

They said _____ are going out.

c   "You should switch off your computer before you go home."

My boss told _____ that _____ should switch off _____ computer.

d   "Please tell my son to ring me back."

Your father phoned to tell _____ to ring _____ back.

**3** **Put the words in the correct order to make sentences.**

that / it / is / said / Fiona / raining

_Fiona said that it is raining._ _____

a   he / that / hamburgers / doesn't / Rafiq / like / said

_____

b   the lesson / The teacher / in the computer room / the student / that / told / is

_____

c   life / me / My father / about / told / my grandfather's

_____

d   must / worried / me / You / you / tell / if / are

_____

e   leaving / He / 8 / o'clock / me / he / at / told / is

_____

f   She / she / very nice / thinks / teacher / said / is / her

_____

g   say / didn't / a problem / Deva / is / there

_____

*She said she thinks her teacher is very nice.*

## Use in context 2: changing tenses

The next day at work, Hamid is talking to Rafiq. Read the conversation. Look at the words in **bold**.

**Hamid**

**Rafiq**

**Hamid:** Did you go to college last night, Rafiq?

**Rafiq:** No, I didn't. The college phoned and told Deva that the heating **had broken down** and so they said there **wasn't** a class for me. They said **they couldn't give** me another class this week. They told me **there would be** an extra class next week instead.

**A** Look at the examples in the table below and write the missing words in the *Reported speech* column.

**Note:** In reported speech, if the information in the message is not fresh and recent, we often change tenses into a past form.

| Rules | | Examples | |
|---|---|---|---|
| Direct speech | Reported speech | Direct speech | Reported speech |
| is/are | <u>was/were</u> | "There isn't a class." | They said there wasn't a class. |
| has/have | _____ | "The heating has broken down." | They told Deva that the heating had broken down. |
| will | _____ | "There'll be an extra class." | They said there would be an extra class. |
| can | _____ | "We can't give you a class." | They said they couldn't give me a class. |
| like (present simple) | _____ | "I like curry." | I told her I liked curry. |

## Practice

**1** **Circle the correct option.**

"I've just arrived." He said he *was* / *had* just arrived.

a "It's started raining." She told me it *was* / *had* started raining.

b "He's going to university in September." She said he *was going* / *has gone* to university in September.

c "I can't speak English very well." He told me he *wouldn't* / *couldn't* speak English very well.

d "We always go on holiday to Egypt." She said they always *went* / *had gone* on holiday to Egypt.

e "I'll see you next weekend." He said he *would* / *could* see me next weekend.

f "I don't want to go out." She said she *hadn't wanted* / *didn't want* to go out.

g "They won't be here till teatime." He told me they *couldn't* / *wouldn't* be here till teatime.

h "I like my class at college." He said he *would like* / *liked* his class at college.

**2** Complete the reported speech sentences with the correct past tense forms.

"I can play the piano." She said _____ she could _____ play the piano.

a "I'll see you next week." He told me _____ see me next week.

b "I've never been to India." She said _____ never been to India.

c "I'm going to have a holiday" He told me _____ going to have a holiday.

d "We've got married." They told me _____ got married.

e "I don't like football." She told me that _____ like football.

f "I won't be home for dinner." He said _____ be home for dinner.

g "I don't think I'll take the exam." She told me that _____ take the exam.

**3** Last week, a student called Carlos told you about his college work. Complete the reported speech sentences.

"I always do my homework."

Carlos told me _he always did his homework_____.

a "I go to college two evenings a week."

He said _____.

b "I can't write English very well."

He said _____.

c "I like my teachers."

He told _____.

d "I've studied English for three months."

He said _____.

e "I don't like using computers."

He told _____.

f "I'm going to university next year."

He said _____.

g "I haven't taken any English exams."

He told _____.

*He said he wouldn't be home for dinner.*

## Use in context 1: simple reported questions

Read the conversations. Look at the words in bold.

**Hamid**

Hamid phones Rafiq. Rafiq is out at work and Deva answers the phone.

**Hamid:** When will Rafiq be home, Deva? Can he phone me back? Thanks.

When Rafiq comes in, Deva gives him the message.

**Deva:** Hamid phoned. He wanted to know **when you would be home**. He asked me **if you could phone him back**.

**Deva**

💡 **How do we make simple reported questions?** (page 85)

**A** Complete the sentences from Deva's message. Notice how the word order changes.

| Type 1 (*Wh~* question words) | "When will Rafiq be home?"<br><br>He wanted to know _____<br><br>_____. |
|---|---|
| Type 2 (*yes/no* questions) | "Can he phone me back?"<br><br>He asked me _____<br><br>_____. |

## Practice

**1** Choose the correct pair of words from the box to complete each pair of reported questions.

> ~~if/when~~    if/how    what time/if    how long/if    if/where    what/if

She asked me ____*if*____ the class started at 9 o'clock.

She asked me ____*when*____ the class started.

a   He asked me _____ I had studied English.

   He asked me _____ I had studied English for long.

b   She wanted to know _____ I lived near the college.

   She wanted to know _____ I lived.

c   He asked her _____ she travelled to work by car.

   He asked her _____ she travelled to work.

d   They wanted to know _____ I got up on Sundays.

   They wanted to know _____ I got up late on Sundays.

e   She asked me _____ I would like to drink.

   She asked me _____ I would like tea with milk.

**2  Put the words in the correct order to make reported questions.**

He asked … I / me / lived / where / .

_He asked me where I lived._

a   She wanted to know … any / if / had / I / children / .

_____

b   He asked … anything / doing / was / she / if / on Saturday / her / .

_____

c   The policeman wanted to know … in / arrived / I / when / had / this country / .

_____

d   My boss asked … late / if / could / me / work / I / .

_____

e   Jeya asked … what / Sundays / she / up / on / got / her friend / time / .

_____

f   Magda asked … Poland / ever / had / I / if / visited / me / .

_____

g   She wanted to know … her / knew / I / if / sister / .

_____

**3  The college secretary has asked you some questions. Complete the reported questions.**

"Do you live in London?"

She asked me _if I lived in London_____.

a   "Can you spell your name, please?"

She asked me _____.

b   "Are you married?"

She wanted to know _____.

c   "Can I see your passport?"

She asked me _____.

d   "How long are you going to stay here?"

She asked me _____.

e   "When will you leave the college?"

She wanted to know _____.

f   "Have you studied English before?"

She asked me _____

_____.

g   "Have you got a visa?"

She asked me _____

_____.

_She wanted to know if I was married._

# Use in context 2: other types of reported question

Deva is at the doctor's. The receptionist is asking her some questions. Read what she says.

**Receptionist**

**Receptionist:** What's your address, please?
And can you tell me your phone number?
Can you just fill in this form for me, please?

When Deva gets home, she tells Rafiq about the receptionist's questions. Look at the words in bold.

**Deva**

**Deva:** She asked me **for my address**.
She wanted to know **my phone number**.
She asked me **to fill in a form**.

 **What other ways of making reported questions are there?** (page 85)

**A** Complete these sentences with words from Deva's message.

| | |
|---|---|
| **Type 1** (specific things) | "What's your address, please?"<br>She asked me _for my address_ . |
| | "Can you tell me your phone number?"<br>She wanted to know _____ . |
| **Type 2** (requests) | "Can you just fill in this form for me, please?"<br>She asked me _____ . |

## Practice

**1** **Four of these sentences are correct and four are wrong. Tick (✓) the ones that are right and correct the mistakes.**

The receptionist asked me for my name. ✓

a   He wanted to know my friend's address.

_____

b   She asked me to directions to the post office.

_____

c   She asked me to phone her this evening.

_____

d   He wanted to know for the best way to London.

_____

e   The police asked me my driving licence.

_____

f   She asked me to lay the table.

_____

g   She asked me for helping her write a letter.

_____

**2** Jan is registering at the college. Match the secretary's questions with the reported questions.

a "What's your name?"

b "How do you write that?"

c "How old are you?"

d "Where do you live?"

e "What do you do?"

f "Who's your next of kin?"

g "Can we contact you on this number?"

h "Please sign here."

1 She asked me for my address.

2 She wanted to know my age.

3 She asked me for my signature.

4 She asked me to check my phone number.

5 She asked me to spell it.

6 She wanted to know my name.

7 She wanted to know my job.

8 She wanted to know my nearest family member.

**3** Make reported questions using one of the forms above.

"Have you got a cigarette, please?"

He asked me _for a cigarette_____.

a "Can you open the window, please?"

She asked me _____.

b "Have you got the time?"

She wanted to _____.

c "Please could you phone the doctor?"

He asked her _____.

d "Could you get some shopping for me, please?"

She asked him _____.

e "Have you got a pencil?"

He asked me _____.

f "Please don't tell anyone my secret."

She asked me _____.

g "How old are you?"

He wanted to know my _____.

*He wanted to know the best way to London.*

## Use in context: *~ing (swimming)*, *to ~ (to swim)*, or *~~to~~ ~ (swim)*?

Read Ling's story. Look at the words in **bold**.

Ling

" When I was a child I always **enjoyed** playing in the water, but I didn't **learn** to swim until a few months ago. At first I didn't **want** to get my hair wet, but now I **don't mind** putting my head under the water.

I **go** swimming at least once a week and I **can** swim quite well. I find it **easy** to swim on my front, but I'm not very good **at** swimming on my back. I **should** do more exercise, so I **would like** to go to the pool more often, but it's **difficult** to get there. I **hope** to get a car soon and then I'**ll** drive there. "

**A** Circle all the *~ing, to ~* and *~~to~~ ~* forms after the words in bold in Ling's story.

**B** Complete these sentences from the conversation.

1 after some words we use *~ing* (gerund):

   I'm not very good at _Swimming_ .

2 after other words we use *to ~* (infinitive):

   I hope _____ a car.

3 after modal verbs we don't use *~~to~~ ~* (infinitive without *to*):

   I can _____ quite well.

**C** Write the bold words from the story in the correct place in the table.

| Words + *~ing* | Words + *to ~* | Words + *~~to~~ ~* |
|---|---|---|
| Verbs:<br>enjoyed | Verbs: | Modal verbs: |
| Prepositions: | Adjectives: | |

For more information on verb forms, see page 90.

## Practice

**1** Complete the sentences with a word from the box. Then add each word to the correct place in the table above.

> expect  important  could  before  ~~stop~~  expensive  must

'Please _stop_ talking and listen to me!'

a I normally have a good breakfast _____ going to work.

b I _____ to change my job next month.

c It's _____ to speak a lot if you want to learn English.

d Clothes are quite _____ to buy in Britain.

e It _____ rain this afternoon but I don't think it will.

f You _____ phone your mother immediately!

**2** **After some words you can use ~*ing* and *to* ~. Read these two paragraphs. Look at the words in bold.**

I **prefer to go** to the pool before work. I really **like to swim** in the early morning before anyone else is around. I usually **start swimming** before 7.30. I **love to have** the pool to myself. I don't **like going** to the pool on Sundays. I really **hate being** there when there are lots of children around.

I **prefer going** to the pool before work. I really **like swimming** in the early morning before anyone else is around. I usually **start to swim** before 7.30. I **love having** the pool to myself. I don't **like to go** to the pool on Sundays. I really **hate to be** there when there are lots of children around.

**Now write the missing verbs to complete the rule:**

• After ___prefer___, _____, _____, _____ and _____ we can use either ~*ing* or *to* ~. (**Note:** After *would prefer*, we use *to* ~.)

**3** **Circle the correct option.**

I don't mind (*staying*) / *to stay* at home tonight.

a  Would you like *having* / *to have* a cup of tea?

b  She enjoys going *shopping* / *to shop* every Saturday afternoon.

c  You should *to buy* / *buy* your train ticket on the Internet.

d  How about *meeting* / *to meet* for a drink tonight?

e  Is it possible *buying* / *to buy* stamps in a supermarket?

f  When will you finish *preparing* / *to prepare* the dinner?

g  I prefer *working* / *work* in the morning rather than in the evening.

h  She offered *helping* / *to help* me write the letter.

i  Is your flat cheap *renting* / *to rent*?

j  I may *to phone* / *phone* my sister tonight.

k  He forgot *giving* / *to give* me your message.

l  You really need to stop *smoking* / *to smoke*.

m  I'm not very keen on *playing* / *to play* tennis this afternoon.

**4** **Work with a classmate. Ask and answer these questions.**

a  What do you hate doing?
b  What are you good at doing?
c  What do you find easy to do?
d  What things are expensive to buy in this country?
e  What do you hope to do in the next 12 months?

f  What do you want to do in the longer-term future?
g  What do you think is important to do if you want to learn English well?
h  When did you start to learn English?

**For example:**

A:  *What do you enjoy doing?*
B:  *I enjoy meeting friends and going out for a meal.*

**5** **Use the words in the box to ask and answer questions. Use ~*ing*, *to* ~ or *~to~* after the word.**

| should | interested in | hate | would like | before | start | go ~ing | hope | forget |
|---|---|---|---|---|---|---|---|---|
| | can | bad at | difficult | important | prefer | mind | | |

**For example:**

A:  *Is it difficult to learn English grammar?*

# Verb forms 2
## some other uses of ~*ing* and *to* ~ verb forms

### Use in context 1: Using ~*ing* (gerund) as the subject of a sentence

Roman is a student from Lithuania. Read what he says about life in Britain. Look at the words in **bold**.

Roman

" **Living** here in Britain is an interesting experience. It isn't always easy. I mean, **driving** on the left is very strange. And **understanding** British people is sometimes difficult, especially when they talk fast. So, **making** new British friends takes time. "

**Note:** In Unit 13 we looked at verbs followed by ~*ing* forms. We also often use ~*ing* forms as the subject of a sentence. (page 86)

**A** **Complete the answers to these questions with words from Roman's story.**

1 What takes time for Roman?

   _making_____ new British friends

2 What's an interesting experience for him?

   _____ here in Britain

3 What's very strange?

   _____ on the left

4 What's sometimes difficult?

   _____ what British people say

## Practice

**1** **Put the words in the correct order to make sentences.**

quite / in Britain / expensive / living / is

_Living in Britain is quite expensive._

a   is / difficult / writing / me / in English / for

_____

b   can / bad / health / smoking / for / your / be

_____

c   tired / night / makes / working / me / at

_____

d   water / good / you / is / drinking / for / very

_____

e   than / is / by / flying / train / faster / travelling

_____

f   at / good fun / college / studying / is / and / interesting

_____

g   necessary / mobile / in / switching off / your / is / the cinema / phone

_____

**2** Rewrite these sentences using ~*ing* as the subject.

It is quite expensive to live in Britain.

<u>Living in Britain</u> _____ is quite expensive.

a  It is lovely to go swimming in the summer.

_____ is lovely in the summer.

b  It is good for you to drink a lot of water.

_____ is good for you.

c  It helps improve your language skills to speak English.

_____ helps improve your language skills.

d  It makes my eyes tired to use the computer a lot.

_____ my eyes tired.

e  It is a cheap form of travel to ride a bike.

_____ travel.

f  My favourite hobby is to listen to music.

_____

g  It is possible for me to get up late on Sundays.

_____

**3** Write sentences about the following topics, using ~*ing* words.

> working in Britain    studying at college    driving on the left    shopping in Britain
> making friends with British people    understanding English    keeping fit    learning English

<u>Living in Britain is more expensive than living at home.</u> _____

_____

_____

_____

**4** Work with a classmate. Ask and answer questions.

**For example:**

A:  *What do you think about living in Britain?*
B:  *Living here is more expensive than at home, but getting a job is easier.*

*Going swimming is lovely in the summer.*

# Use in context 2: Using *to ~* (infinitive) to give reasons

Roman talks about why he came to Britain.
Read what he says. Look at the words in **bold**.

Roman

❝I came to Britain, firstly, **to learn** English and secondly, **to get** a better job.

I go to evening classes at college **to improve** my English.❞

**Note:** We can use *to ~* to give reasons why we do something. We don't use *for* (*for learning English, for to learn English*).

**A** **Complete the answers to the questions using phrases from Roman's story.**

1 Why does Roman go to evening classes?

_____ his English

2 Why did he come to Britain?

_____

English and _____

a better job.

## Practice

**1** **Four of these sentences are correct and four are wrong. Tick (✓) the ones that are right and correct the mistakes.**

I went to the chemist's to get some paracetamol. ✓

I came to Britain ~~for practising~~ my English.

<u>I came to Britain to practise my English.</u>

a I'm working hard to save enough money to buy a car.

_____

b I phoned home last night for to tell my parents some important news.

_____

c She took the dog for a walk getting some fresh air.

_____

d I changed the bathroom tap to stop a leak.

_____

e I looked in the newspaper for see what's on television.

_____

f We went to the travel agent's to book a flight.

_____

g She's gone to the town centre to meet her friends.

_____

h For to get to work, I always take the bus.

_____

**2** Complete the sentences with the correct *to ~* form from the box.

> to become    to meet    to get    to call    to tell    to have
> to lose    to see about    ~~to buy~~    to make

You should try using the Internet ___to buy___ cheap train tickets.

a  She's just gone outside _____ a cigarette.

b  I went to the doctor's _____ my headaches.

c  I've gone on a diet _____ some weight.

d  I rang the dentist's _____ an appointment.

e  I'm studying at university _____ an engineer.

f  I've started jogging _____ fit.

g  I've sent a text _____ him my news.

h  Ring 999 _____ an ambulance.

i  I'm going to the pub _____ my friends.

**3** Think of answers to these questions using *to ~* forms. Then work with a classmate to ask and answer the questions.

**For example:**

A: *Why do people go to the gym?*
B: *They go to the gym to get fit, to lose weight, to feel healthier, to look better and to meet people.*

a  Why did you decide to come to Britain?

_____

b  Why is it necessary for you to learn English?

_____

c  Why do you have a mobile phone?

_____

d  Why are you saving your money?

_____

e  What are your personal goals for the next 12 months?

_____

*I've started jogging to keep fit.*

# Modal verbs 1
## obligation and advice

## Use in context 1: obligation

Jeya is talking to her friend Moona at college.
Read the conversation. Look at the words in **bold**.

Jeya

Moona

**Moona:** Jeya, you **mustn't** forget your ID card, it's really important for security.

**Jeya:** Oh yes, I **need** to get an ID card. Do you know what I **have to** do?

**Moona:** Well, first you **must** go to the office to get a copy of your enrolment form and then you **need to** take that to the Learning Centre.

**Jeya:** Oh right. **Do** I **have to** get any photos? At my last college I **had to** take two photos with me.

**Moona:** No, you **don't have to**. The machine does it for you.

For more information on modal verbs, see page 86.

**A** **Complete these sentences with words from the conversation.**

**Saying something is necessary to do:**

**Statement:**

1 Do you know what I _have  to_ do?

2 Well, first you _____ go to the office …

3 Then you _____ _____ take that to …

**Question:**

4 _____ I _____ _____ get any photos?

**Past form:**

5 I _____ _____ take two photos with me.

**Something it is not necessary to do:**

6 No, you _____ _____ _____.

**Something it is necessary *not* to do:**

7 Jeya, you _____ forget your ID card.

## Practice

**1** **Circle the correct option.**

It isn't raining, so I (*don't have to*) / *mustn't* take an umbrella.

a When I was younger I *had to* / *must* wear a school uniform.

b You *don't have to* / *mustn't* use your mobile phone in the cinema.

c In my present job I *have to* / *had to* start work at 7.00 am.

d Do I *have to* / *must* fill in a form to register at the college?

e Erika is catching the bus, so we *mustn't* / *don't have to* pick her up.

f I *didn't have to* / *mustn't* get a visa to come to this country.

g Did you *need to* / *must* go to work last weekend?

**2** **Write one correct word in each space.**

My wife's expecting to hear from me – I ___*must*___ phone her.

a   She has _____ do her homework tonight.

b   You can wear a suit if you like, but you don't _____ to.

c   Last year, I _____ to change my car.

d   You _____ bring food into the classroom!

e   Do you need _____ get any shopping?

f   We _____ to queue for two hours to get tickets for the concert last night.

g   _____ you have to work this evening?

h   I shall be a long time, so you _____ have to wait for me.

i   Please sit down. I _____ to have a talk with you.

**3** **Write some sentences about the following topics.**

Your schooldays:

● subjects you had to study

   <u>I had to study Maths, Science, History and Geography. We didn't have to study English.</u>

● things you had to do

_____

● things you couldn't do

_____

● qualifications you had to get

_____

Your present and future situation:

● reasons you need to study English

_____

● exams you have to do

_____

● things you have to do here

_____

● things you mustn't do here

_____

**4** **Now work with a classmate. Ask and answer questions.**

**For example:**

A: *What subjects did you have to study at school?*

B: *I had to study Maths, Science, History and Geography. We didn't have to study English.*

*Last year I had to change my car.*

## Use in context 2: advice

Ismail is talking to his teacher at college about a problem. Read the conversation. Look at the words in **bold**.

**Ismail**

**Teacher**

**Ismail:** I have to go back to my country for a month, so I'll miss college. I'm not sure what I **should do**.

**Teacher:** You **ought to go** to the office now and make sure you tell them.

**Ismail:** I'm worried that it might be longer than a month.

**Teacher:** Well, **you could phone** the college from home. You **must take** the number with you.

**Ismail:** **Should I register** for the exam before I go?

**Teacher:** Yes, **I would**. That **would be** best.

For more information on modal verbs, see page 86.

**A** **Complete these sentences with words from the conversation.**

**Asking for and giving advice:**

1   I'm not sure what I ____should do____.

2   You _____ to the office now.

3   _____ for the exam before I go?

**Giving ideas:**

4   Well, _____ the college from home.

**Saying what is the best thing to do:**

5   Yes, _____.

6   That _____ best.

**Giving very strong advice:**

7   You _____ the number with you.

## Practice

**1**   **Match the problem on the left with the advice on the right.**

a   I don't think it's going to rain. Do you?

b   Do you think it's best to tell her the truth?

c   When's the last date for my application?

d   Is the film any good?

e   Do you think I ought to call the doctor?

f   I'm not sure what I should do for my school project.

g   I really don't want to drive to London.

h   The date on this meat is last week. Should we cook it anyway?

1   No, I wouldn't. I'd throw it away.

2   I think you should phone if the symptoms get worse.

3   Well, we could go by train instead.

4   You must make sure it's in by Friday.

5   Well, you could write about your time in Africa.

6   Well, you ought to take an umbrella, just in case.

7   Yes, you must see it – you'd love it!

8   Yes, I would. I think she ought to know.

**2 There are five mistakes in this conversation. Find the mistakes and correct them.**

Student: Can you help me? I'm not sure which level of exam I ~~would~~ take. *should*

Teacher: Well, I think you ought to take the exam you are sure to pass.

Student: But how do I know? Must I see some exam papers, please?

Teacher: Yes, that's a good idea. I would get you some to look at. You should try to do them under exam conditions.

Student: OK, ought I do them here at college in the Learning Centre?

Teacher: Yes, you would. That would be best.

**3 Prepare some advice for visitors to your country. Write some sentences about the following.**

- the best time to visit

  *I wouldn't come in the summer. It's too hot. You ought to come in the spring.*

- the things to do before they come

  _____

- the clothes to bring

  _____

- the best way to travel around

  _____

- where to stay

  _____

- things to do while they are in the country

  _____

- things they shouldn't do

  _____

**4 Work with a classmate. Ask and answer questions.**

**For example:**

A: *Should I come to your country in the summer?*

B: *No, I wouldn't. It's too hot. You ought to come in the spring.*

*You should bring warm clothes.*

# 16 Modal verbs 2
## future possibility and requests

## Use in context 1: future possibility

Amir and Surinder are talking. Read their conversation. Look at the words in **bold**.

Amir

Surinder

**Amir:** What about Abdul's party tomorrow night? **I think I'll** go. How about you?

**Surinder:** I'm not sure. **I might** come… but **I'll probably** have to look after my sister's baby. She's ill at the moment and **I'm pretty certain she won't** be better, but **I could** ring you to let you know.

**Amir:** Yeah, that would be good. You've got my number. So, **I may** see you there, then?

**Surinder:** Well, **I'll definitely** come if I can. **I'll certainly** let you know, anyway.

For more information about modal verbs, see page 86.

**A** Saying how possible something is in the future. Complete these sentences with words from the conversation.

**Saying something is (almost) certain:**

1  I _'m pretty certain she won't_ be better.

2  Well, _____ come if I can.

3  _____ let you know, anyway.

**Saying something is *probable*:**

4  _____ go.

5  _____ have to look after my sister's baby.

**Saying something is *unsure*:**

6  I'm not sure. _____ come

7  _____ ring you to let you know.

8  So, _____ see you there, then?

## Practice

**1** **Three of these sentences are correct and three are wrong. Tick (✓) the ones that are right and correct the mistakes.**

We'll certainly go away in August. ✓

~~I probably may start~~ English classes next month. _I may start/I will probably start_

☐ a  They might move home in the autumn. _____

☐ b  The hotel won't definitely take small children. _____

☐ c  I could send her an e-mail to let her know the news. _____

☐ d  I won't probably be able to see you tomorrow. _____

☐ e  The show will definitely begin at 8.00. _____

☐ f  Surinder want be at the party tonight. _____

**2  Rewrite these sentences using the correct form of** *will, may, might, could* **or** *won't.*

Our team is certain to win the match.  *Our team will definitely win the match.* _____

a   I can definitely say I'll finish the job tomorrow.

I _____ the job tomorrow.

b   Perhaps she'll see him tomorrow.

She _____ tomorrow.

c   I'm not sure if it's going to rain later.

It _____ later.

d   It's probable that I'm not going to take the new job.

I _____ the new job.

e   Maybe she is single, but I don't think so.

She _____ single.

f   He is uncertain about buying a new car.

He _____ a new car.

g   He is certain not to pass the exam.

He _____ the exam.

**3  Write some sentences about yourself using** *will, won't, may, might* **or** *could.* **Use the ideas in the box.**

> go out tonight   do at the weekend   move home   get married   have a family
> stay at college   continue studying English   go to university   get a job   change job
> stay in Britain   go back to your country

_____

_____

_____

_____

_____

**3  Work with a classmate. Ask and answer questions.**

**For example:**

A:  *Do you think you'll go out tonight?*
B:  *No, I probably won't. I may stay in and do the ironing.*

*I'm pretty certain I won't take that new job.*

## Use in context 2: requests

Hamid is in the High Street. A young man stops him and asks him some questions. Read the conversation. Look at the words in **bold**.

Interviewer

**Interviewer:** Excuse me, sir. **Do you mind if I** take a little of your time? It's for a survey.

**May I** ask you a few questions?

... Thank you. **Can you** tell me your name, please?

... Right. **Could I** ask you to spell that for me?

... OK, and **may I** ask how old you are?

... Fine. Now, **could you** tell me where you live?

... And **can I** ask what you do for a living?

Thanks very much indeed, sir.

For more information on requests, see page 87.

**A** **Complete these sentences with words from the conversation.**

**Requests**

**Asking if it's OK to do something:**

1  <u>Do you mind if I</u> take a little of your time?

2  _____ ask you a few questions?

3  _____ ask you to spell that for me?

4  _____ ask what you do for a living?

**Asking someone to do something or for information:**

5  _____ tell me your name, please?

6  _____ tell me where you live?

## Practice

**1** **Three of these requests are correct and four of them are wrong. Tick (✓) the ones that are right and correct the mistakes.**

~~Do I can~~ go to the toilet, please?

<u>Can I go to the toilet, please?</u>

a  Please could you to help me with this suitcase?

_____

b  Can you possibly make a copy of this letter for me?

_____

c  Please may you answer the phone?

_____

d  Could I ask you something about the homework, please?

_____

e  Mind you if I open this window?

_____

f  Could you tell me where can I buy some stamps?

_____

g  Can I get you anything to eat?

_____

## 2 Put the words in the correct order to make requests.

the radio / Do / on / mind / if / I / you / have

Do you mind if I have the radio on _____?

a your / I / pen / May / please / borrow

_____?

b with / this / you / please / me / help / letter / Can

_____?

c give / I / report / you / tomorrow / Could / the

_____?

d me / tell / is / time / what / the / Could / please / you

_____?

e you / why / ask / you / this / if / I / you / country / came / mind / to / Do

_____?

## 3 You go to a very expensive restaurant. Use *can*, *could* or *may* to ask the waiter the following.

sit near the window

Excuse me, could we sit near the window? _____

a see the menu

_____

b have a look at the wine list

_____

c bring some iced water

_____

d change your knife and fork

_____

_____

e close the window

_____

_____

f use the phone

_____

_____

g tell you where the toilets are

_____

_____

*Excuse me, could we sit near the window?*

## Use in context 1: Subject pronouns – *who / which / that / whose*

Antonio has just come back from holiday. He is showing Rafiq some of his photos. Read what he says. Look at the words in **bold**.

Antonio

This is the waitress **who** served us at the café.

Here's a picture of the local bus **that** went round the island.

This is the friend **whose** family lives on the island.

For more information on relative pronouns, see page 87.

**A** We use relative pronouns to connect two ideas. Look at these examples. Complete Antonio's sentences with the correct relative pronouns.

1 This is a waitress. She served us at the café.

This is *the* waitress ___who___ ~~she~~ served us at the café.

2 Here's a picture of a local bus. It went round the island.

Here's a picture of *the* local bus _____ ~~it~~ went round the island.

3 This is a friend. His family lives on the island.

This is *the* friend _____ ~~his~~ family lives on the island.

**Note:** We don't repeat the second subject pronoun (*she, it, his*). Also, *a* often changes to *the*.

**B** Write the missing relative pronouns in these rules.

1 We can use _____ or *that* for people.

2 We can use *which* or _____ for things.

3 We use _____ to show possession (*of who*).

## Practice

**1** Circle the correct relative pronoun.

The man *which* / *who* lives next door is a doctor.

a This is the car *which* / *who* has had a new engine.

b A carpenter is someone *who* / *which* works with wood.

c A duck is a bird *that* / *who* lives near water.

d This is my friend *which* / *whose* brother is a doctor in Africa.

e I've got a tooth *whose* / *that* is very painful.

f That's the actor *whose* / *who* is married to a famous pop star.

g I don't know some of the people *who* / *what* work in my company.

## 2 Correct the mistake in each of these sentences.

Architects are people who ~~they~~ design buildings.

_Architects are people who design buildings._

a Don't forget to pick up your bag which it is under the chair.

_____

b My friend is someone whose knows a lot about computers.

_____

c This is the student that's mobile phone was stolen.

_____

d I like food which it is hot and spicy.

_____

e The police car who passed me was going to an accident.

_____

f The girl that she is standing by the door thinks she knows you.

_____

g Do you know the student that purse was stolen?

_____

## 3 Connect the two sentences using _who, which, that_ or _whose_.

She always wears T-shirts. The T-shirts are too big for her.

_She always wears T-shirts which are too big for her._

a I looked at the clock on the wall. The clock was broken.

_____

b This is a friend of mine. Her daughter got married last Saturday.

_____

c My boss is a manager. She is responsible for the company's finances.

_____

d They are building some new houses. The houses are very expensive.

_____

e We met a writer at the party. Her books are very famous.

_____

f I spoke to someone on the phone. The person told me I had the wrong number.

_____

g Dogs are animals. They can be very intelligent.

_____

## Use in context 2: *where*

Antonio

Here are two more of Antonio's photos.

❝ This is the house **where** my friend lives … and this is the beach **where** we had a barbecue every evening. ❞

For more information on *where*, see page 87.

We can use *where* to connect two ideas about a place. Look at the changes:

1   This is a house. My friend lives there.

This is *the* house *where* my friend lives ~~there~~.

2   This is a beach. We had a barbecue there every evening.

This is *the* beach *where* we had a barbecue ~~there~~ every evening.

**A  Here is another photo. What could Antonio say?**

This is a pool. We sunbathed there all day.

_____ where

_____ .

## Practice

**1  Connect the two sentences with *where*. Put *where* in the position marked \*.**

The hotel\* was very modern. We stayed there.

*The hotel where we stayed was very modern.*

a   There are lots of mountains in the country\*. I live there.

_____

b   She put her jewellery in a secret place\*. Nobody could find it.

_____

c   That's a restaurant\*. They serve really good fish there.

_____

d   The office\* is in the city centre. I work in the office.

_____

e   The pub* was very noisy. We went there.

_____

f   The market* comes to town every Saturday. I get my vegetables there.

_____

g   The airport* was very small. The plane landed there.

_____

**2** **Look at these holiday pictures. Complete each sentence with *This is …* *who / which / that / where*.**

This is the souvenir that _____ cost me a lot of money.

a   _____ took us round the island.

b   _____ we landed.

c   _____ taught us how to windsurf.

d   _____ served us drinks every evening.

e   _____ was our tour guide.

f   _____ was in the town centre.

g   _____ we went swimming every day.

## Use in context 1: object pronouns – when *who / that / which* is not necessary

Antonio

Antonio is showing Rafiq two of his photos. Read what he says. Look at the words in **bold**

1 This is the waitress **who served us** at the café.

2 This is the house **I visited**.

**A** Here are two more of Antonio's photos. Read what he says. Can we take out *who* or *that*?

3 This is the girl **who** I met on the island.

4 Here's a picture of the local bus **that** went round the island.

💡 Notice that in 2 *which / that* is not necessary. Do you know why? Check the notes on page 87.

## Practice

**1** Is *who / that / which* necessary in these sentences? If not, cross it out.

I'm really pleased with the watch ~~that~~ I had for my birthday.

a The phone number that you gave me isn't correct.
b Have you met the new student who has just arrived?
c I prefer the weather which we have in my country.
d I can't remember the name of the teacher who taught us last week.
e She's got a new mobile phone which has lots of different functions.
f She is someone who I have known for ten years.
g She loved the flowers which he gave her.

**2** **Join a phrase on the left with a phrase on the right to make a sentence with a relative clause. Use a relative pronoun from the box if necessary.**

which    that    who    ~~who~~

| | | | |
|---|---|---|---|
| a | My teacher is the one | 1 | is broken. |
| b | The police arrested a man | 2 | gave me a test on my first day. |
| c | This is the computer | 3 | live next door to you? |
| d | I've lost the notebook | 4 | I've had so much trouble with. |
| e | Do you know the people | 5 | is just around the corner. |
| f | I want to sell the old car | 6 | they thought was acting strangely. |
| g | She takes her children to the school | 7 | the company has just employed. |
| h | He is one of the new people | 8 | I keep all my information in. |

a   My teacher is the one *who gave me a test on my first day.* _____

b   The police arrested a man _____

c   This is the computer _____

d   I've lost the notebook _____

e   Do you know the people _____

f   I want to sell the old car _____

g   She takes her children to the school _____

h   He is one of the new people _____

*The police arrested a man they thought was acting strangely.*

# Use in context 2: *where*; prepositions

**In Unit 17, Antonio showed Rafiq some photos of different places. He said:**

This is the house **where** my friend lives.

In sentences with the relative pronoun *where*, we can leave out *where*, but we have to add a preposition. (**Note:** We normally say *live **in** a house*.)

- This is the house where my friend lives.
- This is the house *my friend lives in*.

**A** **Complete the sentence.** (**Note:** We normally say **on** a beach.)

- This is the beach *where we had a barbecue* every evening.
- This is the beach we had

  _____

  every evening.

Many verbs are followed by prepositions: *get on, get off, look for, listen to, talk to*, etc.

We must remember to include these prepositions when we use relative pronouns:

- The bus went round the island. We *got on* the bus.
- The bus (*that*) *we got on* went round the island.

## Practice

**1** **Three of these sentences are correct and four are wrong. Tick (✓) the ones that are right and correct the mistakes.**

That's the hospital where he had his operation. ✓

a  The town I live in is by the sea.

_____

b  Victoria is the station where you arrive at.

_____

c  The place where I parked costs £1.50 per hour.

_____

d  The café what we went to is on the High Street.

_____

e  This is the school my children go at.

_____

f  The room where I work in hasn't got any windows.

_____

g  I liked Italy the best of all the countries we went to.

_____

**2** **Write two different ways of connecting these sentences in the position marked *.**

That's a restaurant*. We first met in that restaurant.

  1  That's the restaurant <u>where we first met</u>.

  2  That's the restaurant <u>we first met in</u>.

a  That's a house*. I lived in that house for ten years.

  1  That's the house where _____ for ten years.

  2  That's the house _____ for ten years.

b  This is a company *. I work for this company.

  1  This is the company where _____.

  2  This is the company _____.

c  This is a street*. She lives on this street.

  1  This is the street where _____.

  2  This is _____.

d  This is a bus stop *. I wait at this bus stop.

  1  This is the bus stop where _____.

  2  This is _____.

e  The university* is very old. I study at that university.

  1  The university where _____ is very old.

  2  The university _____.

f  The mosque* is in the city centre. He goes to this mosque.

  1  The mosque where _____.

  2  The mosque _____.

g  The supermarket* is open 24 hours. I do my shopping at this supermarket.

  1  _____.

  2  _____.


**3** **Talk about your life. Make some sentences using these ideas. Then ask and answer questions with a classmate.**

the people you live with                the place you live in
the student you sit next to             the college you study at
the schools you went to                 the people you go out with
the place you work at                   the people you work with
the music you like listening to         the music you like dancing to
the TV programmes you enjoy watching    the things you like talking about

**For example:**

A:  *Can you tell me about the people you live with?*
B:  *The person I live with is twenty-four years old. He is someone who comes from the same country as me. He is my oldest friend.*

## Use in context

Read about Jeya. Look at the words in **bold**.

Jeya

"I work in my local supermarket. I come here every day **but** I only work in the mornings **as** I've got two young children to look after. **Although** the pay isn't very good, I like working here **because** I can do part-time **and also** my colleagues are nice **and** friendly. **Also**, it's near my home, **so** I can easily walk here **or** catch a bus. "

For more information on linking words, see page 87.

**A** Now complete this paragraph with the correct linking words from Jeya's story.

Jeya works at the supermarket every day, _____but_____ she only works in the mornings <sup>a</sup>_____ she has young children to look after. <sup>b</sup>_____ the pay isn't very good, she likes her job <sup>c</sup>_____ she can do part-time hours <sup>d</sup>_____ her colleagues are nice <sup>e</sup>_____ friendly. <sup>f</sup>_____, it's near her home, <sup>g</sup>_____ she can easily walk there <sup>h</sup>_____ catch a bus.

## Practice

**1** Circle the best linking word for these sentences.

She phoned me *also* / *as* / (*and*) told me her news.

a He works at night *because* / *also* / *although* he earns more money.

b She needed some stamps *or* / *so* / *also* she went to the post office.

c He plays the guitar *but* / *although* / *and* he sings.

d Would you like a break *so* / *also* / *or* do you want to continue working?

e I enjoyed the TV programme *or* / *although* / *also* I didn't understand everything.

f The washing machine's broken. *But* / *As* / *Also*, the toaster doesn't work.

g I'm feeling very tired, *so* / *because* / *although* I don't think I'll go to the party.

**2** Look at these sentences. Choose one linking word that is correct for each pair.

I have tea _____and_____ toast for breakfast.

She works in the morning _____and_____ looks after her children in the afternoon.

a She hasn't got a car _____ she goes to work by bus.

He had a bad cold _____ he didn't go to college.

b I like playing tennis _____ at the moment I've got a bad leg.

He wants to buy a car _____ he hasn't got enough money.

c Would you prefer tea _____ coffee?

I'd like to get a job as a nurse _____ maybe I'll study to be a doctor.

d _____ I live in London, I've never seen the Queen.

I still have problems with my English grammar _____ I've lived here for a long time.

e They decided to stay in _____ the weather was really bad.

She has to leave class early _____ she collects her children from school.

f I enjoy watching comedies. _____, I like thrillers and romantic films.

He's got car problems. It needs new tyres and _____ the brakes aren't very good.

## 3 One linking word in each sentence is wrong. Correct each sentence.

Are you staying long ~~and~~ are you just here for a short holiday? _or_

a I wasn't here last week although I was visiting my family in Bradford. _____

b He doesn't eat ham but he can't eat pork or bacon. _____

c He speaks three languages: English, French or Arabic. _____

d You've still got a temperature because I think you should go to the doctor's. _____

e So the flight was very long, we had a great time in Florida. _____

f They played really well, as they still didn't win. _____

g We'll stop now so it's time to finish. _____

## 4 Fill each gap in the text with an appropriate linking word.

Yesterday, I had to work late __because__ the office was really busy, a_____ I didn't get home till 8 o'clock. I decided to go out b_____ get something to eat c_____ I didn't want to cook. d_____, I didn't have much in the fridge – just an egg e_____ some old lettuce. f_____ I walked round the town centre g_____ there was only one fast-food place open. I had a hamburger h_____ chips i_____ I don't usually eat meat. I didn't enjoy it much, j_____ I don't think I'll eat there again.

## 5 Write some sentences about your life. Try to join them using linking words.

**For example:**

*I go to college. Speaking English is really important for me. – I go to college <u>because</u> speaking English is really important for me.*
*I like Britain. I was lonely when I first came here. – I like Britain <u>although</u> I was lonely when I first came here.*

_____

_____

_____

_____

_____

_____

_____

# 20 The definite article
## *the*

### A Place names

Read what Hamid says. Look at the words in **bold**.

**6 6** I come from **Islamabad** in **Pakistan**. It's a big country in **Asia,** next to **India**. In **the northeast** of the country there are **the Himalayas**, the largest mountain range in the world.

I came to **Britain** six months ago. I live in **Hurst Road, Crawley**, not far from **Gatwick Airport**. I study **English** at **Central Sussex College**. I like **the United Kingdom,** but it's very different from **Pakistan**. **9 9**

**A** Do we normally use *the* before these place names? Write *Yes* or *No* (page 87).

__No__ towns and cities (Islamabad, Crawley)

1 _____ countries and continents (Pakistan, India, Britain, Asia)

2 _____ mountain ranges and rivers (Himalayas)

3 _____ north, south, east, west of a place (northeast of the country)

4 _____ roads and streets (Hurst Road)

5 _____ airports and stations (Gatwick Airport)

6 _____ colleges, schools, universities (Central Sussex College)

7 _____ the names of States, Republics, Kingdoms, Organisations (United Kingdom)

### B Expressions with and without *the*

Read what Hamid says about life in Britain. Look at the words in **bold**.

**6 6** I work part-time, five afternoons a week, as a porter at Crawley Hospital. I leave **home** after **lunch** and I get to **work** at 2.00 pm. I enjoy my work but I feel sorry for all the people in **hospital**. I leave work at 6.00 pm and go straight to **college**. I don't get home until about 9.30 pm and then I generally watch **television** or listen to **the radio** before I go to **bed**. At **the weekends** I like to go to **the cinema**. **Next year**, I hope to go to **university** to study **computing**. **9 9**

**B** Now read these sentences and circle the correct option. (page 87)

We go *to bed* / *to the bed* when we are tired.

1 We stay *in hospital* / *in the hospital* when we are very ill.

2 Most people are *at work* / *at the work* during the day and go *home* / *to the home* at night.

3 We have *lunch* / *the lunch* at 1.00 pm and *dinner* / *the dinner* at 7.00 pm.

4 You have to go to *university* / *the university* to study *medicine* / *the medicine*.

5 In the evening, some people watch *television* / *the television*, listen to *radio* / *the radio* or go to *cinema* / *the cinema*.

6 We say *next* / *the next* month and *last* / *the last* week.

## C General and specific nouns

Read what Hamid says about his diet. Look at the words in **bold**.

❝I'm a vegetarian so I don't eat **meat**. I normally eat **rice** and **vegetables**, cooked with **spices**. I have **fruit** after my meal. I normally drink **water** or **cola** and I never have **alcohol**. I don't think **the food in Britain** is very healthy. Everything is cooked in **fat**, or has **salt** or **sugar** in it. Everyone eats **chips** and **crisps**. It's very bad for **the children in this country**.❞

### 🄲 Now read these statements and cross out *the* if it is incorrect.

Hamid doesn't eat ~~the~~ meat.

1 He eats the rice and the vegetables.

2 He doesn't drink the alcohol.

3 He doesn't like the food here in Britain.

4 In Britain, the food has a lot of the fat, the salt or the sugar in it.

5 The children here in Britain have an unhealthy diet.

## Practice

**1** Look at these place names. Write *the* where it is necessary.

_the_ British Isles

a _____ Scotland

b _____ river Thames

c _____ Manchester Airport

d _____ Alps

e _____ European Union (EU)

f _____ Northern Ireland

g _____ Antarctica

h _____ west coast of America

i _____ Eastern Europe

j _____ Globe Theatre

k _____ Irish Republic

l _____ Oxford University

m _____ Victoria Station

n _____ city centre

o _____ southeast Asia

**2** Are these sentences correct? Tick (✓) the ones that are right and correct any mistakes.

He's in hospital after a serious operation. ✓    I don't normally have ~~the~~ breakfast.

a It's best not to drink beer at lunchtime.

b I'm going skiing in Alps the next week.

c My favourite meal is steak and chips.

d Young people don't usually like the classical music.

e Her husband is in the prison for murder of her mother.

f I got home at about 2.00 am this morning and went straight to bed.

g Instead of watching television, the last night we went to cinema.

h Less than 20% of school leavers go to university.

**3** Look at the words in the box. With a classmate, ask and answer questions with: *Do you like ...?* or *Are you interested in ...?*

> cooking    shopping    the college library    salad    chocolate    films    parties
> football    the English diet    opera    cars    the shops in Britain

For example:

A: *Do you like the college library?*    B: *Are you interested in opera?*

# 21 Adjectives 1
## comparatives and superlatives

## Use in context

Rafiq is a taxi-driver from Sri Lanka. He is talking about Britain. Read what he says.

Rafiq

"When I first came to this country I lived in London, <u>the biggest</u> and busiest city I've ever seen in my life. Now I live near Crawley, about 50 kilometres from London. Of course, a big city is more exciting but, for me, Crawley is better because it's smaller and more peaceful than London.

The furthest north I've been is to Manchester. It's certainly livelier than Crawley! There are many parts of Britain I'd like to visit. People say that Scotland has some of the most beautiful countryside, but also some of the worst weather. There's more rain and less sunshine in Scotland than in England!"

**A** Underline all the comparative and superlative adjectives Rafiq uses.

**B** Complete the examples in the table with adjectives from Rafiq's story.

| Adjective | Comparative (+ *than*) | Superlative |
|---|---|---|
| small | smaller | the smallest |
| big | bigger | ____ _____ |
| peaceful | ____ _____ | the most peaceful |
| exciting | ____ _____ | the most exciting |
| beautiful | more beautiful | __ ____ _____ |
| busy | busier | the _____ |
| lively | _____ | the liveliest |
| good | _____ | the best |
| bad | worse | ____ _____ |
| far | further/farther | ____ _____ |

💡 **Do you know the rules? See Appendix D for more information.** (page 91)

## Practice

**1** Write the comparative and superlative forms of these adjectives.

large     <u>larger</u>     <u>the largest</u>    f expensive ____ ____

a near ____ ____     g bad ____ ____

b happy ____ ____    h sad ____ ____

c far ____ ____    i slim ____ ____

d interesting ____ ____    j friendly ____ ____

e careful ____ ____    k safe ____ ____

**2  Correct the mistake in each of these sentences.**

It's ~~more colder~~ today than yesterday.                                    _colder_ _____

a   This is one of the prettyest villages in England.                         _____

b   The weather in Britain is weter than in my country.                       _____

c   The Nile is the longer river in the world.                                _____

d   She is the most famous person than I've ever met.                         _____

e   I think my English is getting worst!                                      _____

f   New York is moderner than London.                                         _____

g   Have you heard latest news?                                               _____

h   Anna is more friendlier than her husband.                                 _____

**3  Complete the sentences comparing two things. Use comparatives of the adjectives.**

Britain and India

Britain _is smaller and colder than_ _____ India. (*small*, *cold*)

India is _hotter and more mountainous than_ _____ Britain. (*hot*, *mountainous*)

a   A tortoise and a tiger

A tortoise is _____ a tiger. (*slow*, *old*)

A tiger is _____ a tortoise. (*fast*, *young*)

b   Life in the city and life in the country

Life in the city is _____ life in the country. (*busy*, *exciting*)

Life in the country is _____ life in the city. (*calm*, *peaceful*)

**4  Complete the sentences comparing more than two things. Use superlatives of the adjectives.**

a   New York, Cairo, Rome (*busy*, *old*, *attractive*, *romantic*, *big*, *modern*, *rich*)

1   New York is _the richest and most modern_ capital city.

2   Cairo is _____ capital city.

3   Rome is _____ capital city.

b   The lives of a doctor, a film star, a street cleaner (*difficult*, *dirty*, *interesting*, *well-paid*, *interesting*, *rewarding*, *bad*, *badly paid*)

1   A doctor has _____ job.

2   A film star has _____ job.

3   A street cleaner has _____ job.

**5  Write some sentences comparing life in your country with life in Britain. Use comparative and superlative adjectives.**

_____

_____

_____

**6  Now work with a classmate. Ask and answer questions.**

For example:

A:   *How does your country compare with Britain?*

B:   *Well, life in Britain is busier and faster than in my country. Life in my home town is slower – it's the friendliest place I know.*

# 22

# Adjectives 2
*less*, *a lot* / *a bit*, (*not*) *as ~ as, too ~, ~ enough*

## Use in context 1: *less, a lot* / *a bit*, (*not*) *as ~ as*

Read what Rafiq says. Look at the words in bold.

**Rafiq**

❝ When I first came to Britain I worked as a cleaner in a hotel. Now I'm a taxi-driver. Driving taxis is **a lot more interesting than** cleaning hotel rooms. The work is **much better paid** and **far less dirty** than before. Also, I can get up **a bit later** in the morning! So my life now is **not as hard as** when I first arrived here. In fact, I think it's **as good as** it could be! ❞

**A** Read the rules in the table. Complete the examples in the table with the comparative forms from Rafiq's story.

| When we use *less ~ than*, the adjective does not change: | |
|---|---|
| hard | less hard than |
| dirty | less _dirty_ than |
| interesting | less interesting than |

| When we use (*not*) *as ~ as*, the adjective does not change: | | |
|---|---|---|
| good | _____ good _____ it could be |
| hard | not _____ _____ _____ |
| dirty | not as dirty as |
| interesting | not as interesting as |

| When we use *a lot, far, much, a bit*, and *a little*, the adjective changes to the comparative form: | | |
|---|---|---|
| hard | a little | harder |
| interesting | _____ | more _____ |
| late | _____ | _____ |
| dirty | _____ | less _____ |
| well-paid | _____ | _____ paid |

## Practice

**1** **Circle the correct option.**

Their new car is ⟨*not as big as*⟩ / *not so big than* their old one.

a My new job is *a bit better paid than* / *a little well-paid than* my old one.

b My younger sister is *as tall as* / *as taller as* me.

c Their house is *much less cleaner than* / *much less clean* than ours.

d My country is *a lot beautiful than* / *a lot more beautiful than* Britain.

e I think tennis is*n't as interesting as* / *more interesting as* football.

f Her boyfriend is *far younger than* / *far younger as* her ex-husband.

g A Jaguar is *so comfortable as* / *as comfortable as* a Mercedes.

**2  Write one word in each space to complete the sentences.**

Being a cleaner is ___*less*___ well-paid than being a taxi-driver.

a  My town is less noisy _____ London.

b  Learning English is a _____ easier than learning Chinese.

c  New York is _____ more modern than London.

d  A Ford is not as fast _____ a Ferrari.

e  My sister is just a _____ older than me.

f  My brother's job is far _____ important than mine.

g  I get up a little _____ on Sundays – around 10 o'clock.


**3  Rafiq is looking at three houses. Look at the information.**

|         | Built in | Number of bedrooms | Location      | Price    |
|---------|----------|--------------------|---------------|----------|
| House 1 | 1990     | 1                  | city centre   | £210,000 |
| House 2 | 1990     | 2                  | by the airport| £220,000 |
| House 3 | 1850     | 5                  | in the country| £475,000 |

**Write some sentences about the houses with *far, a lot, much, a bit, a little, (not) as ~ as.*
Use the adjectives in brackets.**

House 3 is _*much older than*_____ the other two. (*old*)

a  House 1 is as _____ house 2. (*modern*)

b  House 2 is a bit _____ house 1. (*large*)

c  House 1 is not as _____. (*interesting*)

d  The location of house 2 is much _____. (*noisy*)

e  The location of house 1 is not _____. (*peaceful*)

f  House 1 is _____. (*cheap*)

g  House 3 is _____. (*expensive*)

*My sister is just a little older than me.*

# Use in context 2: *too / enough*

Rafiq has looked at the three houses in exercise 3 on page 69. Read what he says about them. Look at the words in **bold**.

**Rafiq**

" I liked house 1 because it was**n't too expensive** for me, but it was**n't big enough** for my wife and baby. House 2 was **big enough** for us and it was **cheap enough** for me to buy, but it was by the airport so it was **too noisy**. House 3 was certainly **large enough** for us, but it was **far too expensive**. Also it was **too old** and it was**n't near enough** to the city centre. "

 **How do we use *too* and *enough*?** (page 87)

**A** Which is correct? Tick (✓) the correct rule.

1 We normally use:

  a   *too* + adjective (e.g., *too noisy*) ✓

  b   adjective + *too* (e.g., *noisy too*)

2 We normally use:

  a   *not* + *too* + adjective (e.g., *not too expensive*)

  b   *not* + adjective + *too* (e.g., *not expensive too*)

3 We normally use:

  a   *enough* + adjective (e.g., *enough big*)

  b   adjective + *enough* (e.g., *big enough*)

4 We normally use:

  a   *not* + *enough* + adjective (e.g., *not enough near*)

  b   *not* + adjective + *enough* (e.g., *not near enough*)

## Practice

**1** **Put the words in the correct order to make sentences.**

It / cold / to go / too / swimming / was

*It was too cold to go swimming.*

a   isn't / enough / old / school / He / to leave

_____

b   is / enough / She / a model / beautiful / to be

_____

c   a bit / to buy / The car / is / expensive / for me / too

_____

d   short / for her / to work / to wear / too / The skirt / was

_____

e   our English / The lessons / to practise / enough / aren't / for us / long

_____

**2** Write a sentence with *too* or *enough* for each of these situations.

She can't drive. She's only 15.

She isn't <u>old enough to drive.</u>

a You've arrived late. You can't do the exam.

You've arrived _____

b I didn't go to the party. I was really tired.

I was _____

c The car was cheap. We could buy it.

The car was _____

d The bag was heavy. I couldn't carry it.

The bag was _____

e Your writing isn't clear. No one can read it.

Your writing isn't _____

f She is not very well, but she can still go to school.

She is _____

g He won't get the job. He has no experience.

He isn't _____

**3** Write some sentences about your family or country using *too*, *enough* and the ideas below.

| ... too | hot    cold    old    young<br>expensive    small    big    tired | to ... |
|---------|---------------------------------------------------------------|--------|
| ... not | hot    cold    old    young<br>cheap    good    clever    big | enough to ... |

<u>In my country, it's too hot to play football and tennis.</u>

_____

_____

**4** Now ask and answer questions with a classmate.

**For example:**

A: *In your country, is it too hot to play sports in the summer?*

B: *It's too hot to play football and tennis, but we play cricket.*

*The car was cheap enough for us to buy.*

# 23

# Quantity
*some, any, much, many, a lot (of), a few, a little, all, most*

## Use in context

Read the conversations. Look at the words in bold.

Rafiq

**Rafiq:** I'm going out. Do you need **any** shopping?

**Deva:** I don't need **a lot,** but you could get me **some** eggs and **a few** apples.

**Rafiq:** Have you got **any** cash?

**Deva:** Just **a little**. How **much** cash do you need?

**Rafiq:** About £20.

Deva

**Doctor:** How **many** cigarettes do you smoke?

**Ismail:** Well, I used to smoke a lot, but now … **not many**. Maybe ten a day.

**Doctor:** Really you shouldn't smoke **any** at all.

Doctor

💡 **How do we use *some* and *any*?**
(page 88)

**A** Complete the rules and examples with the correct word from the conversations.

| | We use | Examples |
|---|---|---|
| **Questions** | _____ | Have you got _____ cash? |
| **Negative statements** | *any* | You shouldn't smoke _____ cigarettes at all. |
| **Affirmative statements** | | You could get me _____ eggs. |

Ismail

💡 **How do we use *much, many, a few, a little*?** (page 88)

**B** Complete the rules and examples with the correct word from the conversations.

| | We use | Examples |
|---|---|---|
| **Uncountable nouns** | *much* _____ | How _____ cash do you need? Just _____ . |
| **Countable nouns** | _____ _____ | How _____ cigarettes do you smoke? You could get me _____ apples. |

**Note:** We can use *a lot (of)* with countable and uncountable nouns, in affirmative and negative sentences and questions.

**Ismail:** Do you think people from your country find it difficult to live in England?

**Rafiq:** Well, in any new country **most** people have a problem with the language or finding a job but **most of the people** I know have now got a job. **Some of them** have got two jobs. Also, **all of my** friends are studying English at college. So, things soon get better.

💡 **When do we use *all of, most of, some of*?**
(page 88)

**C** Complete the words and examples with the correct word from the conversations.

| We use... | | before these words. | Examples |
|---|---|---|---|
| All | | the, this, these, that, those | _____ people I know have now got a job. |
| _____ | *of* | my, your, his, her, its, our, their | Also, *all of my* friends are studying English at college. |
| _____ | | me, you, him, her, it, us, them | _____ have got two jobs. |

# Practice

**1** **Circle the correct option.**

I haven't got *some* / (*any*) money.

a   We saw *some* / *any* friends yesterday.
b   How *much* / *many* coffee do you drink?
c   I only like *a few* / *a little* sugar in my tea.
d   Have you had *some* / *any* e-mails today?

e   We eat *many* / *a lot of* Indian food.
f   "Do you know *many* / *much* people here?"
     "No, not *much* / *many* … only *a few* / *a little*."
g   There is *much* / *a lot of* traffic in our street.

**2** **Complete these sentences with *some*, *any*, *much*, *many*, *a lot* (*of*), *a few*, or *a little*.
There may be more than one possible answer.**

How ____many____ euros are there in ten pounds?

a   I don't eat _____ sweets.

b   We had _____ rain overnight.

c   There are _____ messages for you on the answerphone – three, I think.

d   I've got _____ homework to do, but not _____.

e   I don't think we had _____ post yesterday.

f   You need to earn _____ money to buy a house.

g   "Are there _____ people from your country in the college?"

     "No, not _____, only _____."

**3** **Three of these sentences are correct and three are wrong. Tick (✓) the ones that are right
and correct the mistakes.**

Most ~~of~~ people in Africa are poor.  *Most people*
Some of the students in my class passed their exams.  ✓

a   All of cities are very noisy.

b   Some my best friends are British.

c   I feel happy most of the time.

d   Most children enjoy their schooldays.

e   I had some of the sweets, but not all them.

f   All Hollywood film stars earn a lot of money.

**4** ***of* or *~~of~~*?**

Most _of_ the students came to my party.

a   Our teacher spoke to all _____ us.

b   Most _____ mobile phones are also cameras.

c   How do you spend most _____ your weekends?

d   I like listening to all _____ good music.

e   There were some _____ things in the lesson that I didn't understand.

f   Some _____ these eggs aren't fresh.

g   China now produces most _____ the electrical goods you can buy.

h   Most _____ oranges come from Spain.

i   Please turn off all _____ mobile phones.

# 24 Prepositions of time

## Use in context

The teacher is giving the class information about the exams. Look at the words in **bold**.

Teacher

**Teacher:** The exams are **in June**. Your exam will probably be **on Tuesday the 22nd**, **in the evening**. The exams start **at 5.30**.

💡 **How do we use *in*, *on*, *at* with different expressions of time?**

**A** Look again at what the teacher says and complete these rules with the correct preposition.

| a month<br>the morning/evening<br>a period of time from now<br>a season<br>a year<br>a decade<br>a century<br>~ the middle of … | in | ~ June<br>~ the evening<br>The lesson ends ~ ten minutes.<br>~ spring<br>~ 2007<br>~ the 1990s<br>~ the eighteenth century<br>~ the middle of winter |
| a day or part of a day<br><br>a date<br>a special day | ____ | ~ Tuesday<br>~ Tuesday evening<br>~ 22nd June<br>~ New Year's Day |
| a time<br>night<br>the weekend<br>the moment<br>a festival<br>~ the beginning/end<br>　of something | ____ | ~ 5.30<br>~ night<br>~ the weekend<br>~ the moment<br>~ Christmas<br>~ the beginning/end of<br>　the lesson |

The teacher gives some more information. Look at the words in **bold**.

**Teacher:** Well, the speaking and listening exam lasts **for** about 20 minutes. Your exam is **from** 5.30 **till** about 5.50. I'm sure you'll finish **by** 6 o'clock. **While** you are talking to your partner, the examiner will listen. You can make notes **during** the exam.

💡 **How do we use *for*, *from ~ till ~*, *by*, *while*, *during*?**

**B** Complete these rules with the correct preposition from the information.

**To talk about:**

1　the **latest** time when something finishes:

I'm sure you'll finish ___by___ 6 o'clock.

2　when something **starts and finishes**:

Your exam is _____ 5.30 _____ about 5.50.

3　a **period of time**:

the exam lasts _____ about 20 minutes.

4　something that happens **at the same time as** something else:

*with verb*: _____ you are talking to your partner, the examiner will listen.

*with noun*: You can make notes _____ the exam.

## Practice

**1** Correct the mistake in each of these sentences.

We change the clocks ~~in~~ the beginning of winter.　　　___at___

a　I'm going to London in the weekend.　　　_____

b　We have four days' holiday on Easter.　　　_____

c　I sometimes do my homework in the night after work.　　　_____

d　Britain had two wars on the twentieth century.　　　_____

e　I'll be ready at five minutes.　　　_____

**74** | Unit 24 – Prepositions of time

f  I like to sit and relax in the end of the day.  _____

g  I have to get up early in Monday morning.  _____

## 2  Use *in*, *on* or *at* to complete the following phrases.

<u>on</u>  2nd July

a  _____ 14.15

b  _____ 1953

c  _____ New Year's Day

d  _____ the morning

e  _____ spring

f  _____ midnight

g  _____ Friday afternoon

h  _____ an hour's time

i  _____ the 1900s

j  _____ December

k  _____ the end of the day

l  _____ Christmas Day

m  _____ the moment

n  _____ Sunday night

o  _____ half past ten

p  _____ Ramadan

q  _____ the 1940s

r  _____ November 5th

s  _____ Valentine's Day

t  _____ a week's time

u  _____ a quarter to six

v  _____ the sixteenth century

w  _____ the middle of the lesson

## 3  Complete these phrases with the best preposition: *for, from ~ till ~, by, while, during.*

<u>from</u>  Monday  <u>till</u>  Friday

a  _____ the picnic

b  _____ about three hours

c  _____ the TV programme

d  _____ 2.30

e  _____ three weeks

f  _____ morning _____ night

g  _____ the TV was on

h  _____ a very long time

i  _____ the football match

j  _____ three _____ five

k  _____ I was going to work

l  _____ midday on Friday

m  _____ the end of the week

## 4  Correct the mistakes in these sentences. Use *for, from ~ till ~, by, while, during.*

She was really tired ~~for~~ the end of the week.  <u>by</u>

a  She listened to the news during she was having breakfast.  _____

b  The evening class is for 6 o'clock by 9 o'clock.  _____

c  She had to go out during the film was showing.  _____

d  You must finish the report till this afternoon.  _____

e  Someone was eating chips while the film.  _____

f  We're going on holiday during three weeks.  _____

g  It started to rain by I was walking home.  _____

## 5  Work with a classmate. Ask and answer questions about times. Use the prepositions *in*, *on*, *at*, *for*, *from ~ till ~*, *by*, *while*, *during*, with the following ideas:

- routines: daily, weekly, monthly, yearly
- important dates in the past and in the future
- things you must do before a certain time

**For example:**

A:  *When do you normally go on holiday?*
B:  *We normally go away at the beginning of summer, in June or July.*

A:  *What are you going to do at the end of this course?*
B:  *I'm going back to my country at the end of this course.*

# 25 Prepositions
## after adjectives and verbs; prepositional phrases

## Use in context 1: prepositions after adjectives and verbs

Jomo is talking to his teacher. Read the conversation. Look at the words in **bold**.

**Teacher**

**Jomo**

**Teacher:** Are you interested in sport?

**Student:** Well, I'm quite keen on athletics. I believe in keeping fit so I belong to a gym. I'm good at running. I go jogging and listen to music on my iPod at the same time.

**Teacher:** Oh, do you go jogging every day?

**Student:** Well, to be honest, it depends on the weather. I get fed up with running in the rain. I'm not afraid of getting wet, but you have to be dressed in the right clothes.

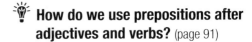 **How do we use prepositions after adjectives and verbs?** (page 91)

**A** **Complete these phrases with words from the conversation.**

Are you interested __in__ sport?

1 I'm good _____ running.

2 I belong _____ a gym.

3 I'm not afraid _____ getting wet.

4 I'm keen _____ athletics.

5 You have to be dressed _____ the right clothes.

6 It depends _____ the weather.

7 I listen _____ music on my iPod.

8 I believe _____ keeping fit.

9 I get fed up _____ running in the rain.

## Practice

**1** **Circle the correct preposition.**

Cheng's job depends *of* / *on* the result of the interview.

a Hamid isn't very keen *on* / *of* English food.

b The train arrives *in* / *to* Paris at 3.15.

c Rafiq is married *with* / *to* Deva.

d Life in my country is very different *of* / *from* life in England.

e I sometimes get fed up *with* / *by* the English weather.

f Ling said she was sorry *about* / *to* arriving late.

g I got *to* / *at* work early yesterday.

h It was very kind *of* / *to* you to help me.

i We should believe *on* / *in* respecting people from different cultures.

j She was dressed all *in* / *with* white for the wedding.

k I'm a little afraid *by* / *of* my neighbour's big dog.

**2** **Match the phrase on the left with a phrase on the right.**

a  Watching TV is very good                         1  with yourself.

b  It's nice to have friends when you arrive         2  for your English.

c  In a foreign country you are afraid               3  on you.

d  If you don't understand, it's easy to be angry    4  at learning languages.

e  It's easier in a foreign country if you're good   5  in yourself.

f  You always remember people who have been kind     6  of saying the wrong thing.

g  Your success in a new country depends             7  to you.

h  You will be successful if you believe             8  in a new country.

**3** **Complete the sentences with the correct preposition.**

My grandfather was very kind __to__ me.

a  It was very kind _____ you to help me.

b  I'm very good _____ learning languages.

c  Drinking lots of water is good _____ you.

d  I'm angry _____ her about what happened.

e  She didn't speak to me because she was angry _____ last night.

f  The plane arrived _____ Gatwick Airport at 10.00 am.

g  They arrived _____ Sri Lanka last week.

h  She was sorry _____ interrupting the lesson.

i  I feel sorry _____ all the victims of war.

*I'm a little afraid of my neighbour's big dog.*

# Use in context 2: prepositional phrases

Read Youssef's story. Look at the words in **bold**.

Youssef

❝ I'm studying music at college. The college is in the centre of town so I usually go by bus, but I can get there on foot if it's a nice day. I like to get to college early in the morning, in time to do some practice before classes start. ❞

🔆 **How do we use prepositions in phrases?**
(page 92)

**A** **Complete the phrases below with words from Youssef's story.**

studying music ___at___ college

1 _____ time

2 get _____ college

3 go _____ bus

4 get there _____ foot

5 _____ the centre _____ town

## Practice

**1** **Circle the correct option.**

He works best **in** / **at** night.

a   We went to Spain **by** / **in** plane.

b   The Principal's office is **on** / **at** the first floor of the building.

c   My friend is **at** / **in** hospital with a broken leg.

d   There was an interesting programme **in** / **on** television last night.

e   **By** / **In** my opinion, nurses should get better salaries.

f   You will find the answer **in** / **at** the bottom of the page.

g   We arrived at the station **in** / **on** time to get a sandwich before the train came.

h   The post office is just round the corner **on** / **in** the right.

i   He was **with** / **in** a suit and a tie for his interview.

j   I usually get **home** / **at home** at around 6.30 pm.

k   She came to England **in** / **at** the same time as me.

**2** **Complete each sentence with the correct preposition.**

Go through the door ___on___ the left.

a   I met some nice people _____ holiday.

b   Cornwall is _____ the west of England.

c   I've never travelled anywhere _____ boat.

d   I spoke to the girl _____ blonde hair.

e   He was _____ prison for five years.

f   I love walking _____ the rain.

g   What's _____ at the cinema?

**h** She often goes away _____ business.

**i** Look at the picture _____ page 17.

**j** I think I saw David Beckham getting _____ a taxi.

**k** She had to leave _____ the middle of the lesson.

**3** **Write sentences about yourself using prepositions with adjectives, verbs and phrases. Look at the words in the boxes for ideas.**

| interested | afraid | angry | different | dressed | fed up | keen |

| arrive | believe | belong | depend | wait | listen |

| bus | holiday | home | hospital | south | time | TV | university |

**For example:**

*I'm afraid of heights.*
*I don't like many programmes on TV.*
*I'm fed up with waiting for buses.*

_____

_____

_____

_____

_____

**4** **Work with a classmate. Ask and answer questions.**

**For example:**

**A:** *What are you interested in?*
**B:** *I'm interested in cooking.*

**B:** *How do you get to college?*
**A:** *I usually go by bus.*

*He was in a suit and tie for his interview.*

**Phrasal verbs**

## Use in context

Read these four sentences. Look at the words in **bold**.

"**Look out**! There's a car coming."

"Sorry, I can't come out tonight. I'm **looking after** my sister's baby."

"I'm really **looking forward to** my holiday."

"You could **look** that word **up** in a dictionary."

💡 **How do we make phrasal verbs?** (page 88)

**A** Complete the sentences with the correct words from above.

<u>Look out!</u> There's a car coming.

1  You could _____ that word _____ in a dictionary.

2  Sorry, I can't come out tonight. I'm _____ _____ my sister's baby.

3  I'm really _____ _____ _____ my holiday. *

*Some phrasal verbs have two particles.

💡 **How do we use phrasal verbs?** (page 88)

**B** Write one of the phrasal verbs with **look** next to each of these meanings.

take care of someone or something <u>look after</u>

1  be excited about something in the future

   _____

2  be careful _____

3  find out information from a book, the Internet, etc. _____

**C** There are three types of phrasal verb (page 92). Complete the examples with the correct words from the sentences above.

| Type 1<br>Phrasal verbs with no object | look <u>out</u>_____ |
|---|---|
| Type 2*<br>Object between (or after) verb and particle | look that word _____<br>(look _____ that word)<br>look it _____ |
| Type 3<br>Object after particle | look _____ my sister's baby<br>look _____ my holiday |

## Practice

**Note:** You can find all the phrasal verbs you need for these exercises on page 92.

**1** **Circle the correct preposition.**

You can look *to* / *up* nearly everything on the Internet.

a  A nurse looks *after* / *for* patients in hospital.
b  You need to fill *in* / *up* a form to register at college.
c  I think it's raining so I'll put *down* / *on* my raincoat.
d  "Could you hold *up* / *on* a moment while I find a pen?"
e  Before you buy a new car you should always try it *out* / *on*.
f  She was busy so I'll have to phone her *back* / *down* later.
g  The TV won't work because you haven't plugged it *on* / *in*.

## 2 Complete each of these sentences with a word from the box.

> in   down   down   away   off   up   up   up   ~~out~~

Remember to look __out__ when you cross the road.

a   Please hurry _____ or we'll be late.

b   I got _____ very early this morning.

c   The plane took _____ at 11.30.

d   I can't hear you so could you speak _____ a little, please?

e   I can't get to work because my car's broken _____.

f   The driver drove _____ from the accident without stopping.

g   Please come _____ and sit _____.

## 3 Circle the correct verb.

I'm (looking) / setting forward to seeing my family again.

a   Do you mind if I switch / get on the TV?
b   You need to take / put on a coat this morning.
c   I look / take after my mother in the way I look.
d   I'll have to put / take off my dentist's appointment because I'm ill.
e   Be careful you don't take / knock over that cup of coffee.
f   I tried to phone you last night but I couldn't get / hold through.
g   I find it difficult to look / work out the meaning of new words.

## 4 Are these sentences correct? Tick (✓) the parts that are right and correct any mistakes.

Plug in the TV ✓ and ~~switch on it~~. _switch it on_

a   Your shoes are wet. Take off them and put your slippers on. _____

b   I drop my kids off at school at 8.15 and pick them up again at 3.30. _____

c   After you've washed the dishes up, dry up them, please. _____

d   I put the phone down when the operator cut off me. _____

e   I'm going to tidy up my room and throw all the rubbish away. _____

f   I'm nearly running petrol out of, so I need to fill the car up. _____

g   I gave up smoking last year but I took up it again after I lost my job. _____

## 5 Work with a classmate. Ask and answer questions using phrasal verbs. Use some of these ideas.

- put on / take off (e.g., clothes)
- take up (e.g., a new activity, a new course)
- take after (e.g., a person in your family)
- run out of (e.g., food, drink, petrol)
- tidy up (e.g., room, house, garden)
- throw away (e.g., old clothes, rubbish)
- look after (e.g., children, elderly people, sick people)
- look forward to (e.g., a holiday, a party, going somewhere)
- give up (e.g., smoking, alcohol, eating meat)

**For example:**

A: *What did you put on to go to work this morning?*   B: *I put on my uniform.*

# Grammar notes

## 1.1 present simple and adverbs of frequency

- To make the *he/she/it* forms (3ʳᵈ person singular) of the present simple, for most verbs, add *-s*: *work → works, listen → listens, drive → drives*

- For verbs ending in *s, sh, ch, tch, x*, add *-es*: *miss → misses, crash → crashes, touch → touches, watch → watches, fix → fixes*

- For verbs ending in a consonant + *y*, add *-ies*: *study → studies, marry → marries*

- Negatives: *I/you/we/they **don't**, he/she/it **doesn't*** + verb (infinitive without *to*): *I **don't** work. She **doesn't** work.*

- Questions: ***Do** I/you/we/they, **Does** he/she/it* + verb (infinitive without *to*): ***Do** you go? **Does** he work?*

- Short answers: *Yes, I **do**./No, I **don't**; Yes, he **does**./No, he **doesn't**.*

## 1.2 present continuous

- To make the present continuous tense, use *I **am**, you/we/they **are**, he/she/it **is** + -ing*: *I **am** work**ing**.*

- We often use contractions: *I'm, you're, we're, they're, he's, she's, it's + -ing*

- Negatives: *I'm not, you/we/they **aren't** ('re not), he/she/it **isn't** ('s not) + -ing*

- Questions: ***am** I, **are** you/we/they, **is** he/she/it + -ing?*

**Spelling of *-ing* forms:**
- For most verbs, add *-ing*: *work**ing**, play**ing**, meet**ing***

- For verbs ending in *-e*: *make → making, write → writing*

- For verbs ending in *-ie*: *die → dying, lie → lying*

- Verbs ending in one vowel + consonant: *cut → cutting, stop → stopping*

- Some stressed syllables: *begin → beginning,* but *open → opening*

**We use the present continuous tense to talk about:**
- things which are happening now: *I'm watching TV now.*

- things happening at the present time: *I'm studying at college at the moment.*

- changing situations: *Prices are going up.*

- and temporary situations: *I'm staying with my brother while I'm in London.*

- We can also use the present continuous to talk about the future. See Unit 2.

- Non-continuous verbs. Some verbs are not normally used in the continuous form. See Appendix B, page 90.

## 2.1 present continuous, *going to, will*

- We make sentences with ***going** + **to*** infinitive. *I am ('m), you/we/they **are** ('re), he/she **is** ('s) **going to** save.*

- Negatives: *I'm not, you **aren't**/you're not, he **isn't** going to save.*

- Questions: ***am** I, **are** you/we/they, **is** he/she/it **going to** save?*

- We make sentences with ***will** ('ll)* + infinitive. *I/you/he/she/it/we/they **will** ('ll) **get**.*

- The negative of *will* is ***won't**.*

- Questions: ***will** I/you/he/she/it/we/they **get**?*

- We can use ***shall** and **shan't** with *I* and *we*: *I **shall** ('ll) go, we **shan't** see.*

- We often use ***shall** in questions with *I* and *we* for offers and suggestions: ***Shall** I give you a ring? **Shall** we meet at 8 o'clock?*

- Note: Sometimes the difference in meaning is very small: *I'm having a meeting with him tomorrow; I'm going to have a meeting with him tomorrow; I'll have a meeting with him tomorrow.*

- Generally, ***going to*** expresses something *you* have personally already decided to do in the future, and the ***present continuous*** is often an arrangement with other people. We often use ***will** for a spontaneous decision we make at the moment of speaking. Also we can use ***will/won't*** to talk generally about the future: *I'll be in Paris next week.*

- We do not use the present simple for future plans and arrangements: *I ~~see~~ him tomorrow.* We can use the present simple for schedules and timetables: *My plane leaves at 10 o'clock.*

## 2.2 more uses of *will, won't, going to*

- We can use **will** when we want someone to believe our promise: *I'll pay you back.* Sometimes, **will** is stressed: *I **will** be home by 10.30.*

- We can also use **will** to predict the future, to say what we think will happen: *In the future, there will be more electric cars; Barcelona will win the European Champions League.*

- We can use **won't** to make a *strong* negative statement of refusal. This may be personal: *I won't tell you the secret.* **Shan't** is also possible with *I* and *we: I shan't do what you say!*

- We can also use **won't** when things go wrong: *The printer won't work.*

- We use **going to** when it is clear from a present situation what is going to happen next: *The doctor examined Deva and told her that she is going to have a baby; Some children are walking to the tennis courts carrying tennis rackets, so they are going to play tennis.*

## 3.1 past simple

- There are two kinds of past simple forms: regular and irregular. The regular forms are:
  - Verb + **-ed**: work**ed**, start**ed**
  - Verbs ending in **-e**, add **-d**: *live* → live**d**, *arrive* → arrive**d**
  - Verbs ending in consonant + *y: carry* → carr**ied**, *stu*d**y** → stud**ied**
  - Verbs ending in vowel + consonant: *stop* → sto**pp**ed
  - Some verbs with stressed syllables: *pre*f**er** → prefe**rr**ed
  - There are three ways of pronouncing *-ed* endings in regular verbs: /t/ *worked,* /d/ *arrived,* /ɪd/ *started.* The pronunciation depends on the last consonant of the verb: /t/ after *s, f, ch, sh, o, p, k, x* and voiced *th*; /d/ after *z, v, w, r, b, m, n, g, l, j* and voiceless *th*; /ɪd/ after *t, d* and *y* (*-ied*).
  - The form doesn't change: *I/you/he/she/it/we/they worked.*

- For a list of common irregular verbs, see Appendix A, page 89.

- We use the past simple to talk about actions which we know are finished: *I came to England three months ago*; or about finished times: *I saw him yesterday.*

## 3.2 past continuous

- We make the past continuous tense with **was/were** + **-ing**: *She **was** talk**ing**.*

- Questions: **was/were** + subject + **-ing**: ***Were** you sitt**ing** in the canteen?*

- Negatives: **wasn't/weren't** + **-ing**: *I **wasn't** watch**ing**.*

- Non-continuous verbs: some verbs are not normally used in the continuous form. See Appendix B, page 90.

- Note: We often use the past continuous when we are telling a story in the past.

## 4 past situations and habits: *used to*

- *I/you/he/she/it/we/they* **used** + **to** infinitive: *I **used to live** with my parents.*

- Negatives: *I/you/he/she/it/we/they* **didn't use** + **to** infinitive: *I **didn't use to work**.*

- Questions: **Did** *I/you/he/she/it/we/they* **use** + **to** infinitive: ***Did you use to go** out to work?*

- Short answers: *Yes, I did.* or *Yes, I used to. No, I didn't.*

- Notice that the form doesn't change: *He used to lives; We used to lived; We used to living; Does she use to live?*

- The pronunciation of *used to* is /juːst tuː/.

- There are other uses of *used to* which are not covered in this book.

## 5 present perfect 1: *Have you ever …? How long have you …?*

- To make the present perfect, we use *I/you/we/they* **have**, *he/she/it* **has** + past participle (3rd form of the verb): *I **have seen**; he **has seen***

- Negatives: *I/you/we/they* **haven't**, *he/she/it* **hasn't** + past participle

- Questions: **have** *I/you/we/they*, **has** *he/she/it* + past participle

- Short answers: *Yes, I* **have**. *Yes, he* **has**. *No, we* **haven't**. *No, she* **hasn't**.

- The verb **go** has two past participles: **been** and **gone**. We use **been** if a person has visited somewhere and returned: *I've **been** to New York twice.* We use **gone** if the person is away at the moment: *Where's Amir? He's **gone** to the bank.*

- We use **for** + a period of time: *for a month;* **since** + time/date: *since Monday*

- The present perfect has a connection with the present. For more uses, see Unit 6.

## 6 present perfect 2: an unfinished timeframe

- These four uses of the present perfect are about a *present result* of a past action. The timeframe of the action has not finished.

- We use the present perfect with **just** to talk about something that happened a short time ago in the past.

- We normally use **yet** in negatives and questions, **already** in positive statements.

- We normally use the present perfect if the time has not finished. For example, *today* – when we are speaking, *today* has not finished: *Has Hamid phoned today?* If the time has finished, we use the past simple. For example, if the time is now 3 o'clock in the afternoon, we say: *Did Hamid phone this morning?*

- Note that American English often uses the past simple with **just**, **yet** and **already** – *I just called to say 'I love you'.* British English uses the past simple only for actions and times that are finished and which have no connection with the present.

- When we speak, we normally use contractions: *I've* (have), *it's* (has)

## 7 present perfect 3: present perfect or past simple?

**Past simple:**

- **Finished time**
  *Did you go there yesterday/last summer?*
  *yesterday/last summer* = We know the time has finished.

- **Finished action or situation**
  *When did you go?* = We know she went and she is not there now.
  *How long did you live in London?* = We know he lived in London but he is not there now.
  *Hamid changed his car last year.* = We know that this is not a new action.

- **Typical words and phrases**
  *When?, What time?, yesterday, last …, ago*

**Present perfect:**

- **Unfinished time**
  *Have you ever been to Scotland?*
  *ever* = at any time in your life, up to now

- **Unfinished action or situation**
  *How long have you been a taxi-driver?* = We know he is still a taxi-driver now.

- **Present result of a past action**
  *I see you've bought a new taxi.* = I can see your new taxi for the first time.

- **Typical words and phrases**
  *ever, never, since, just, already, yet, this …, today*

## 8 sentences with *if* and *when:* zero and first conditionals

- We normally use *zero conditionals* for facts, things which are always true, and sometimes for instructions.

- In zero conditionals, we normally use the present tense after **if**. In the other part of the sentence we also use the present tense: *If you **open** a savings account, you **get** more interest.*

- **When** can replace **if** in zero conditionals without a change of meaning or form.

- We normally use first conditionals for situations which are probable or possible, or with **when**.

- In first conditionals, we normally use the present tense after **if**. In the other part of the sentence, we can use:
  - a modal verb: *If you **go** to the bank, you **can ask** for advice.*
  - an imperative: ***Take** your passport with you if you **want** to open an account.*
  - or a future tense, normally **will/won't**: *If you **go** to the bank, I'll **come** with you.*

- **When** can replace **if** in a first conditional. The sentence has the same form but a different meaning. It becomes something we are sure about and no longer a possibility (conditional): *I'll **let** you know **when** I go.*

- Conditional sentences have two parts, or clauses. We can normally change the position of the two parts: *If you go to the bank, you can ask for advice. You can ask for advice, if you go to the bank.* We normally use a comma when the *if*-clause is first.

## 9.1 *be* as a main verb

- We can use **be** as a main verb: *How old **are** you? I'm 27*; or as an *auxiliary* verb: *What **are** you doing? I'm watching television.*

- Present tense: *I **am**, you/we/they **are**, he/she/it **is***

- We often use contractions: *I'm, you/we/they're, he/she/it's*

- Negatives: *I'm **not**; you/we/they **aren't**; he/she/it **isn't***

- Questions: *am I?*, *are you/we/they?*, *is he/she/it?*

- Past tense: *I/he/she/it* **was**, *you/we/they* **were**

- Present perfect: *I/you/we/they* **have been**, *he/she/it* **has been**

- Future: *I/you/he/she/it/we/they* **will be**

- Note: We use **be** with ages: *How old* **are** *you? I'm 27.*

## 9.2 *have* as a main verb

- We can use **have** as a *main* verb: **Do** *you* **have** *the time? No, I* **don't have** *a watch.*

- We can also use **have** as an *auxiliary* verb with the present perfect: *I* **have** *lived.*

- Present tense: *I/you/we/they* **have(n't)**; *he/she/it* **has(n't)**

- We normally ask questions with **do/does**: *do I/you/we/they* **have?**; *does he/she/it* **have?**

- In the present tense we can also use **have got** to talk about possessions and illness, but not routines or activities: *I've* **got** *a new watch.* **Have got** is usually less formal.

- Past tense: *I/you/he/she/it/we/they* **had**. Present perfect: *I/you/we/they* **have had**, *he/she/it* **has had**

- Future: *I/you/he/she/it/we/they* **will have**

## 10 indirect (embedded) questions

- Notice how the word order changes in an indirect question:
  - In a direct question: *When do the lessons start?*
  - In an indirect question, we use a question (*Can you tell me when?*) + a sentence: (*the lessons start*)**:** *Can you tell me when the lessons start?*

- A verb + preposition normally stay together in an indirect question: *Where does she* **come from?** *Do you know where she* **comes from?**

- There is little difference between **if** and **whether** in indirect questions. In most situations, it does not matter which one we use.

## 11.1 *say* or *tell?*

- It is possible, but not necessary, to use **that** after **say** and **tell**:
  - **She told me** *the heating's broken down and* **she said that** *there's no class this evening.*
  - **She told me that** *the heating's broken down and* **she said** *there's no class this evening.*

- We use a noun or a personal pronoun after **tell**: **tell** *the teacher/me you/him/her/us/them*, etc.

- We do not normally change the tenses in a reported message if the information is still fresh and current.

## 11.2 changing tenses

- We may also have to change some other words, for example, pronouns (*him → you*), places (*here → there*), some verbs (*come → go*), times (*tomorrow → the next day*): "*Please tell him to come here at 10 o'clock tomorrow.*" → *They told* **you** *to* **go there** *at 10 o'clock* **the next** *day.*

## 12.1 simple reported questions

- We can use *wanted to know* or *asked* (+ person) in reported questions.

- For direct questions that begin with a **wh**-question word, we make the reported question with: question word + reported sentence: "*When will he be home?*" → *He wanted to know* **when you would be home**.

- For other questions (with a *yes/no* answer), we normally make the reported question with: **if/whether** + reported sentence: "*Could he phone me back?*" → *He asked me* **if you could phone him back**.

## 12.2 other types of reported question

- When we ask for a specific thing, it is sometimes possible to make the reported question with: **ask** + person + **for** + thing: "*What's your address?*" → *She* **asked me for my address**.

- In conversation, when we are asking for information we can sometimes leave out **for**: *She asked me my address.*

- We use: **want to know** + thing (~~for~~, ~~person~~): "*Can you tell me your phone number?*" → *She* **wanted to know my phone number.**

- When we make a request, we ask someone (not) to do something for us: "*Can you fill in this form for me, please?*" → *She* **asked me to fill in a form for her**; "*Please don't talk in class.*" → *She* **asked them not to talk in class**.

- We can also make reported sentences with **tell** in a similar way: *I* **told** *her my address; She* **told** *me to fill in a form.*

## 13 verb forms 1: ~ing, to ~ or to ~?

- We use the -*ing* form of a verb in several different ways. Here are two of them:
  - in continuous tenses after the verb *be*: *I am* *waiting, she was talking,* etc. This -*ing* form is called the present participle.
  - after some verbs: *I enjoy swimming, they stopped working,* etc.; and after most prepositions: *I'm good at swimming.* This -*ing* form is called the gerund.

- There is no rule in English to explain why we use -*ing* after some verbs and *to* - after other verbs. See Appendix C page 90.

- We often use -*ing* after *go*, for sports and activities: *go swimming, go shopping,* etc. We normally use *to* - after verbs with *would*: *I would like to talk to you.*

- We don't normally use -*ing* after the preposition *to*. Exceptions are *look forward to* and *be used to*: *I'm looking forward to going* on holiday; *I'm used to eating* British food.

- We use *to* - after some adjectives: *It's easy to swim.*

- We don't use *to* - after most modal verbs: *I can swim.* Exceptions are *have to* and *ought to I have to do* my homework; *I ought to phone* my mother.

- For spelling of -*ing* forms: see 1.2.

- Note: Sometimes there can be a small difference in meaning: *I like swimming* (= always, generally); *I like to swim on Sunday mornings* (= a special occasion), but it is not important and English people use both -*ing* and *to* - after these verbs. But remember, we normally use *to* - with *would*: *I'd love to* have a swim; *I'd prefer to* stay in.

## 14.1 verb forms 2: using ~ing (gerund) as the subject of a sentence

- We can use an -*ing* form (gerund) at the beginning of a sentence. It acts like a noun: *Living here in Britain is an interesting experience.*

- In Unit 13, we saw that we can use a *to* - form *after* an adjective. So, we could also say: *It is interesting to live* here in England.
  - *Driving on the left is very strange.* → *It is very strange to drive* on the left.
  - *Understanding English people is sometimes difficult.* → *It is sometimes difficult to understand* English people.

## 15.1 obligation

- To say something is necessary, we use: *have/has to, need to, must to*

- To say something is not necessary, we use: *don't/doesn't have to, don't/doesn't need to*

- To say something was necessary in the past we use: *had to/didn't have to*

- We ask questions: *Do I /Does he have to? Do I/Does he need to? Must I/she to? Did you have to?*

- *Must* is a modal verb and we cannot use it in the past: *musted*

- *Mustn't* means that something is forbidden or prohibited: *You mustn't do it.* = *You are not allowed to do it.* We can say *couldn't* for the past: *We couldn't* smoke at school.

## 15.2 advice

- *Ought to* and *should to* have the same meaning. *Must* has a stronger meaning.

- For negative advice, we can say *shouldn't to* or *oughtn't to,* but we often say: *I don't think you should …, I don't think you ought to …*

- We can ask a question with *should I to?* or *ought I to?* but we often use: *Do you think I should? Do you think I ought to?*

- To make a suggestion, we can use *you could* or *you might*.

- We often use *I would(n't)/I should(n't)* to confirm or reject an idea, meaning: *This is what I would/wouldn't do if were you.* We usually stress *I*: *Well, I would.* We also say: *That would be good/best/a good idea.*

## 16.1 future possibility

- We use *will/won't* to say something is certain in the future.

- We use *may/might/could* to say something is possible. *May, might* and *could* have a similar meaning, but *might* can mean something is a little less possible than *may* and *could*. We can also say *may not* and *might not* (*mightn't*) for a future possibility but do not use *couldn't*: *I may not* see you tomorrow.

- We do not use *to* after *will, won't, may, might* or *could*: *I may to see you.*

- We often use the adverbs *definitely, (almost) certainly, probably* with *will* and *won't*.

- We normally use an adverb *between* **will** and a verb: *I'll* **probably** *come.*

- But we use the adverb *before* **will** in a short answer: *"Will you come tomorrow?"* *"Yes, I* **probably** *will".*

- We normally use an adverb *before* **won't**: *I* **definitely** *won't come./I* **definitely** *won't.*

16.2 requests

- When we ask if it's OK to do something (ask for permission), we can use: **do (would) you mind if** *I …,* or the modal verbs **may** I?, **can** I?, **could** I? There is little difference in meaning – *could I?* is a little more polite than *can I?*; *May I?* is a little more formal.

- We normally only use **may** in requests with the 1ˢᵗ person: **may** I?, **may** we?, not ~~may you?~~ When we ask someone to do something or for information we can use **can you?** or **could you?** We do not use ~~May you…?~~

- We do not use **to** after **can**, **could** or **may**: *Could you* ~~to~~ *close the window?*

17.1 subject pronouns – *who / which / that / whose*

- Note: In American English, **that** is used much more than in British English for **who** or **which**: *This is the waitress* **that** *served us every mealtime.*

18.1 object pronouns – when *who / that / which* is not necessary

- We have to keep **who**, **which** or **that** if it is the **subject** of the following verb. We can usually see it is not necessary if there is a *new subject* of the second verb. Look at the examples.
  - *This is the* **waitress who served** *us at the café.* = *the waitress served us.* Because **waitress** is the subject of *served,* **who** is necessary.
  - *This is the* **house I visited**. = **I** *visited the house.* Because **I** (not the *house*) is the subject of *visited,* **which/that** is not necessary.

19 linking words: *and, also, but, or, so, because, as, although*

- We use linking words to join words, ideas and sentences together.

- We use **as**/**because** + a reason. It answers the question **Why?**

- We use **so** + a result.

- We use **also** to say something extra. We can use **also** at the beginning or in the middle of

a sentence. We can use **and also** in the middle of a sentence.

- We use **although** (and **but**) to join two opposite or contrasting ideas. We don't normally use **but** at the beginning of a sentence.

- We use **and** to connect two similar ideas.

- We use **or** to connect two alternative ideas.

- We don't normally use **and** or **or** at the beginning of a sentence.

20 the definite article: *the*

**A Place names**

- We don't use **the** if we are talking about a region without using **of**: *He is from* ~~**the**~~ *southeast Asia* or **the** *southeast of Asia.*

- We normally use **the** if we are talking about one, special road in a town: **the** *High Street,* **the** *main road*

- We normally use **the** if we are talking about one, special place in our town: **the** *station,* **the** *library,* **the** *post office*

- We use **the** with **of**: **the** University **of** Cambridge. Also, we say **the** Open University, because it is a special university.

**B Expressions with and without *the***

- We don't normally use **the** when we talk about these states: (*be in/go to/get out of*) **bed**, **hospital**, **prison**; (*go to/be at*) **work**; (*go to/be in/at*) **school**, **college**, **university**, **church**; (*go/get/leave*) **home**; (*have/eat*) **breakfast**/**lunch**/**dinner**/**supper**; (*watch*) **television**

- We don't normally use **the** with study subjects and leisure activities: (*play*) **classical music**; (*study*) **medicine**

21 adjectives 1: comparatives and superlatives

- When we compare two things, places or people, we use the *comparative* form of the adjective + **than**: *It's more peaceful* **than** *London.*

- When we compare three or more things, places or people, we use **the** + the *superlative* form of the adjective: **The** *biggest and busiest city I've ever seen.*

22.2 *too/enough*

- We use **too** + adjective, but adjective + **enough**: **too** *expensive, big* **enough**

- After these structures, we often use **for** +

person (*for me*) and/or the infinitive (*to buy*): *It was cheap **enough for me to** buy*; *It was **too** noisy **for us to** live in.*

23 quantity: *some, any, much, many, a lot (of), a few, a little, all, most*

- We use **some** and **any** with uncountable *and* countable nouns: *Have you got **any cash**? You could get me **some eggs**.*

- We normally use **any** in questions: *Have you got **any cash**?* However, we can use **some** if we expect the answer yes: *"Have you got **some cash** for me?" "Yes, you know I've just been to the cash machine."*

- Normally, we don't use **much/many** in affirmative sentences: *I've got **a lot of** cash. I've got **a lot of** eggs.*

- We can use **a lot** if we don't want to repeat the noun: *I don't need **a lot** (of apples).*

- In informal English we can say **lots of**: *I've got **lots of** cash. I've got **lots of** eggs.*

- We can use **a little** or **not much** for small amounts of uncountable nouns.

- We can use **a few** or **not many** for small amounts of countable nouns.

- After **most**, we do not use **of** before general nouns without *the*: **most people**

- We must use **of** with **some/most** if they are followed by **the** or a *pronoun* (e.g., *them*): **most of the** people, **some of them**

- We also say **any/none/enough** + **of** + **the** or a pronoun: **any of the** students, **none of my** friends, **enough of them**

- We can say **all of** or **all** before **the/this** or a pronoun: **all of the** time/**all the** time, **all of this** week/**all this** week, **all of my** friends/**all my** friends

- But we must use **all of** before **us/you/them**: *She spoke to **all of us.***

24 prepositions of time

- We *don't* normally use a preposition before **this/next/last**: *I'm seeing her this Saturday; I'm on holiday next week; I bought a new car last week.*

- We can say **in the beginning/end** for a general meaning if there is no **of** following: *In the beginning, I was quite unhappy; In the end, I was very happy.*

- We can use **from** ~ **till/until/to** ~ with the same meaning: *Your exam is from 5.30 until about 5.50; Your exam is from 5.30 to about 5.50.*

- We use **during** to mean while something is happening: **during** + noun: **during** *the exam* ( = while I was doing the exam).

25 prepositions after adjectives and verbs; prepositional phrases

- After some adjectives and verbs we must use a preposition. We also use prepositions in some English phrases. See Appendix E, page 91 for a list of some of the common adjectives and verbs + prepositions and prepositional phrases.

26 Phrasal verbs

- The prepositions in phrasal verbs are really *adverbial particles* because they are part of the verb. They look like prepositions, but they are not really the same.

- A phrasal verb is a verb + particle(s) with a *special meaning*. Sometimes other verbs are followed by prepositions (*listen **to** music, get **in** the car*) – without a special, extra meaning. These are not phrasal verbs. They are usually called *prepositional* verbs.

- If a phrasal verb has three parts, they are: verb + particle + preposition: **look** + **forward** + **to**.

- We use phrasal verbs a lot in conversations and informal English. Most phrasal verbs also have a more formal equivalent, e.g., *look after = take care of.* See Appendix F, page 92 for a list of common phrasal verbs. Phrasal verbs often have more than one meaning.

- With Type 2 phrasal verbs, if the object is a pronoun (*me, you, him, her, it, us, them*), always put the pronoun *between* the verb and the preposition. If the object is a noun, it can go before or after the particle: *dry the dishes up, dry up the dishes, dry them up, ~~dry up them~~.*

| Infinitive | Past simple | Past participle |
|---|---|---|
| be | was/were | been |
| beat | beat | beaten |
| become | became | become |
| begin | began | begun |
| bite | bit | bitten |
| blow | blew | blown |
| break | broke | broken |
| bring | brought | brought |
| build | built | built |
| buy | bought | bought |
| catch | caught | caught |
| choose | chose | chosen |
| come | came | come |
| cost | cost | cost |
| cut | cut | cut |
| do | did | done |
| draw | drew | drawn |
| drink | drank | drunk |
| drive | drove | driven |
| eat | ate | eaten |
| fall | fell | fallen |
| feed | fed | fed |
| feel | felt | felt |
| fight | fought | fought |
| find | found | found |
| fly | flew | flown |
| forget | forgot | forgotten |
| forgive | forgave | forgiven |
| freeze | froze | frozen |
| get | got | got |
| give | gave | given |
| go | went | gone/been |
| grow | grew | grown |
| have | had | had |
| hear | heard | heard |
| hide | hid | hidden |
| hit | hit | hit |
| hold | held | held |
| hurt | hurt | hurt |
| keep | kept | kept |
| know | knew | known |
| lay | laid | laid |
| lead | led | led |
| leave | left | left |
| lend | lent | lent |
| let | let | let |

| Infinitive | Past simple | Past participle |
|---|---|---|
| lie (1) | lied | lied |
| lie (2) | lay | lain |
| light | lit | lit |
| lose | lost | lost |
| make | made | made |
| mean | meant | meant |
| meet | met | met |
| pay | paid | paid |
| put | put | put |
| read | read | read |
| ride | rode | ridden |
| ring | rang | rung |
| rise | rose | risen |
| run | ran | run |
| say | said | said |
| see | saw | seen |
| sell | sold | sold |
| send | sent | sent |
| set | set | set |
| shake | shook | shaken |
| shine | shone | shone |
| show | showed | shown |
| shut | shut | shut |
| sing | sang | sung |
| sit | sat | sat |
| sleep | slept | slept |
| speak | spoke | spoken |
| spend | spent | spent |
| spread | spread | spread |
| stand | stood | stood |
| steal | stole | stolen |
| stick | stuck | stuck |
| sweep | swept | swept |
| swim | swam | swum |
| take | took | taken |
| teach | taught | taught |
| tell | told | told |
| think | thought | thought |
| throw | threw | thrown |
| understand | understood | understood |
| wake | woke | woken |
| wear | wore | worn |
| win | won | won |
| write | wrote | written |

Here are some common verbs which we do not normally use in the continuous form. These are sometimes called *state* or *stative verbs*.

| Like/Dislike | Mental activity | Senses | Possession |
|---|---|---|---|
| dislike<br>hate<br>like<br>love<br>need<br>prefer<br>want<br><br>(Note: *enjoy* is *not* a stative verb.) | agree<br>appear<br>believe<br>forget<br>know<br>matter<br>mean<br>realise<br>recognise<br>remember<br>seem<br>*think (believe)<br>understand | hear<br>see<br>smell<br>taste<br><br>(We often use *can, can't* with these verbs: *I can't hear you; I can see them.*) | belong to<br>cost<br>*have/have got (possess)<br>own |

\* *think* and *have*: these verbs have two different meanings:
**think**: 1 believe: *I think it's going to rain*; 2 use the brain: *Quiet, I'm thinking right now.*
**have**: 1 possession: *He has two cars*; 2 activity: *Are you having a good time?*

| | |
|---|---|
| **Verbs + *~ing***<br>avoid, consider, dislike, enjoy, finish, go (+ activity – go swimming), imagine, involve, (don't) mind, postpone, practise, stop\* | **Prepositions + *~ing***<br>about, after, at, before, by, for, from, in, off, on, since, with, while |
| **Verbs + *to ~***<br>afford, agree, decide, expect, forget\*\*, help, hope, learn, manage, offer, prepare, promise, refuse, want, would hate/like/love/prefer | **Adjectives + *to ~*** (*I find it … to ~ / It's … to ~*)<br>cheap, difficult, easy, expensive, hard, important, impossible, possible, right, wrong |
| **Modal verbs + *to ~***<br>can, could, may, might, must, should, will, would | |
| **Verbs + *~ing* or *to ~* (the meaning is the same)**<br>begin, continue, hate, like, love, prefer, start | |

\* **stop** + **to** has a different, special meaning.
\*\* **forget** + *~ing* has a different, special meaning.

|  | Adjective | Comparative (+ *than*) | Superlative |
|---|---|---|---|
| 1 Short words of one syllable, add ~*er*, ~*est*. | small<br>old | smaller<br>older | the smallest<br>the oldest |
| 2 With some short words the spelling changes (vowel + consonant = double the last consonant). | hot<br>big | hotter<br>bigger | the hottest<br>the biggest |
| 3 Normally, with two-syllable words, add *more*, *most*. There are a few exceptions. | modern<br>peaceful<br>quiet | more modern<br>more peaceful<br>quieter | the most modern<br>the most peaceful<br>the quietest |
| 4 Two-syllable words ending with ~*y*, use ~*ier*, ~*iest*. | busy<br>lively | busier<br>livelier | the busiest<br>the liveliest |
| 5 With longer adjectives, use *more*, *most*. | exciting<br>beautiful | more exciting<br>more beautiful | the most exciting<br>the most beautiful |
| 6 There are a few irregular adjectives. | good<br>well-paid<br>bad<br>far<br>much/many<br>little/few | better<br>better-paid<br>worse<br>further/farther<br>more<br>less | the best<br>the best-paid<br>the worst<br>the furthest /farthest<br>the most<br>the least |

### 1a prepositions after adjectives

afraid *of*
angry *with* someone
angry *about* something
different *from*
dressed *in*
fed up *with*
good *at*
keen *on*
kind *of*
kind *to*
interested *in*
married *to*
sorry *about* something
sorry *for* someone

### 1b prepositions after verbs

arrive *at* (station/airport/town)
arrive *in* (city/country)
believe *in*
belong *to*
depend *on*
get *to*
listen *to*
talk *to*
wait *for*

**kind of/kind to**: *It was kind **of** you to lend me £50; The nurse is kind **to** her patients.*

| at | study *at* (school/college/university)<br>*at* the (top/bottom)<br>*at* the same time<br>*at* (night/Christmas/the weekend) |
|---|---|
| *in* | to be *in* bed<br>to be *in* (hospital/prison/church)<br>to be *in* (clothes): *He was in a grey suit.*<br>*in* the (north/south/east/west)<br>*in* the (middle/centre)<br>*in* my opinion<br>*in* the (rain/sun)<br>*in* the (morning/evening/afternoon) |
| *on* | to be *on* (business/holiday)<br>What's *on* (TV/the radio/at the cinema)?<br>to be *on* the (phone/computer)<br>to be *on* fire<br>*on* the (right/left)<br>*on* page 15<br>*on* the (ground/first) floor |
| *with* | a person *with* (a physical feature): *the man with a beard* |
| transport | *by* (car/train/bus/plane/ship/bike)<br>*on* (foot/horseback/a camel)<br>*get on/get off* (a bus/train/ship/plane)<br>*get in/get out of* (a car/taxi) |
| *home* | (go/come/arrive/get/leave) *home* |
| time | *on time* = exactly the right time: *She arrived on time at nine o'clock.*<br>*in time* = before the time: *She arrived at five to nine, in time for the meeting.* |

## Appendix F: common phrasal verbs

| Type 1: phrasal verbs with no object | |
|---|---|
| *break down* | a car breaks down when it doesn't work |
| *drive away* | leave a place in a car, bus or truck |
| *get through* | communicate by phone |
| *get up* | get out of bed |
| *hold on* | wait a moment |
| *hurry up* | be quick |
| *look out* | be careful |
| *sit down* | take a seat |
| *speak up* | speak more loudly |
| *take off* | a plane leaves the ground |

| Type 2: object between verb and particle (or after) | |
|---|---|
| *cut off* | a person is cut off during a phone call if the line goes dead |
| *drop off* | take someone somewhere in a car or bus |
| *dry up* | dry dishes and cups, after washing up |
| *fill in* | complete the details in a form |
| *fill up* | put liquid in something until it is full |
| *give up* | stop a habit |
| *knock over* | make something or someone fall down |
| *look up* | find information in a book or on the Internet, etc. |
| *phone back* | return a phone call |
| *pick up* | collect someone by car |
| *plug in* | connect a machine with electricity |
| *put down* | place an object on table or floor, etc. |
| *put off* | postpone, make a later time for a date |
| *put on* | dress in clothes |
| *switch on* | turn on the power |
| *take off* | remove clothes |
| *take up* | start a new hobby, interest, sport, activity, course of study, etc. |
| *throw away* | put in the rubbish bin, get rid of |
| *tidy up* | clean and make order in a place |
| *try on* | try clothes, for size |
| *try out* | test to see if something works |
| *wash up* | wash the dishes |
| *work out* | find the meaning of, or the solution to something you don't understand |

| Type 3: object after phrasal verb | |
|---|---|
| *come in* | enter a room |
| *look after* | take care of something or someone |
| *look for* | try to find something or someone that is missing |
| *look forward to* | be excited about something in the future |
| *run out of* | have nothing left of food, drink, petrol, etc. |
| *take after* | look like or have a similar personality to someone in your family |

# Answer key

## Unit 1.1

**A**  2 works   3 do you go   4 Does he work
5 don't work   6 doesn't go

**B**  1 I usually take   2 we're always

**1**  a does   b flies   c studies   d fixes   e watches
f makes   g plays   h costs   i has   j washes
k pays   l drives   m carries

**2**  a Does; play   b doesn't rain   c Do; use   d talk
e produces   f Do; go   g doesn't cost

**3**  a They usually watch television in the evenings.
b We often see him at the college.
c Do you usually drive to work?
d We don't always go out for lunch on Sundays.
e He sometimes stops at the supermarket on his way home.
f What time does your neighbour get home from work?
g He never answers the phone when I ring.

## Unit 1.2

**A**  2 She's staying   3 are you doing?
4 Is she; working   5 she isn't working
6 I'm not working

**B**  now, still, right now, at the moment

**1**  a getting   b meeting   c trying   d dying
e making   f writing   g sleeping   h arriving
i shutting   j eating   k having   l beginning
m visiting   n happening

**2**  a are screaming   b is getting   c is wearing
d is arriving   e is sitting   f are having   g is trying
h is crying   i aren't getting   j is beginning

**3**  a The sun's shining.   b Is it raining?
c Is she having a shower?   d Are you using the computer?
e The kettle's boiling.   f Are you watching TV?
g The radio isn't working.

**4**  a Is it improving?   b is getting   c I sometimes get
d is getting   e I'm talking   f We all feel
g do you generally study   h I don't usually do
i I don't have   j I'm studying   k I'm trying
l I always find   m do you think   n I believe

## Unit 2.1

**A**  2 We're going to buy   3 I'll ask

**B**  present continuous; will/won't

**1**  a 'm teaching   b 'm marking   c Are   d doing
e 'm driving   f 'm attending   g Are   h doing
i 'm meeting   j 'm   k doing

**2**  a is going to buy   b is going to study
c is going to change   d is going to babysit
c is going to fly   f is going to lose   g is going to try

**3**  b–8; c–4; d–3; e–1; f–7; g–6; h–5

**4**  a I'm going to be   b I'm having; I'm seeing
c I'll try   d I'm going to paint   e I'll go and get

## Unit 2.2

**A**  1 won't start   2 will; 'll have
3 going to; t's going to rain

**1**  b–4; c–7; d–8; e–1; f–5; g–6; h–2

**3**  a 's going to rain.   b 's going to fall off
c 's going to miss   d 's going to have
e are going to cross

## Unit 3.1

**A**  1 didn't know   2 did; come   3 did; do

**B**  Regular: worked, started
Irregular: got, met, began

**C**  1 ✔

**1**  a came   b ate   c bought   d wrote   e closed
f broke   g told   h studied   i left   j paid   k heard
l opened   m flew   n tried   o enjoyed   p caught
q stopped   r taught   s wore

**2**  /t/ watched, walked, helped
/d/ lived, played, loved, called
/ɪd/ shouted, needed, waited, hated

**3**  yesterday, what time?, last week, ago

**4**  a picked   b didn't come   c Did; take
d Did you call   e didn't go; had   f did you have
g didn't buy; didn't have

**5**  a went   b Did   c see   d did   e had   f didn't stay
g had   h hired   i travelled   j Did   k get
l didn't go   m saw   n spent   o swam   p ate
q relaxed

## Unit 3.2

**A**  was, was, were; drinking, having, chatting, sitting

**B**  b–4; c–1; d–2

**1**  a ~~writting~~ writing   b ~~didn't~~ wasn't   c ~~Did you were~~
Were you   d ~~were~~ was   e ~~was~~ were   f ~~rain~~ raining
g ~~wasn't knowing~~ didn't know

**3**  a was still sleeping; came   b was raining; was driving
c came   d hated   e was coming; had
f was reading; was watching

**4**  a decided   b were walking   c started/began
d stood   e was raining   f stopped
g played   h were playing   i began/started   j went
k ordered   l were drinking   m came   n returned
o was playing

**5** **a** was waiting  **b** was raining  **c** was standing
**d** saw  **e** stopped  **f** asked  **g** realised  **h** came
**i** was doing  **j** were chatting  **k** went  **l** stopped
**m** continued  **n** was feeling  **o** started  **p** got
**q** turned  **r** heard

## Unit 4

**A**  **2** Did; use to  **3** did; didn't  **4** didn't use to

**B**  **2** ✔

**C**  **2** used to

**1**  **a** ~~was~~ **b** use  **c** ~~being~~ be
**d** ~~don't~~ didn't  **e** ~~used~~ use  **f** ~~use~~ used
**g** ~~used to have~~ had

**2**  **a** didn't  **b** used to  **c** used to  **d** did you use to
**e** did  **f** used to  **g** used to
**h** didn't use to/never used to  **i** used to  **j** used to

**3**  **a** used to; usually  **b** usually; used to
**c** used to; usually  **d** used to; usually
**e** usually; used to  **f** used to; usually

**4**  **a** didn't use to go  **b** didn't use to have
**c** used to wear  **d** used to travel  **e** used to ride
**f** didn't use to drink

## Unit 5

**A**  have, have, has; lived, phoned, rung

**B**  **2** have; lived

**C**  1–b; 2–a

**1**  **a** bought  **b** got  **c** grown  **d** had  **e** left  **f** lost
**g** seen  **h** been  **i** gone/been  **j** met  **k** thought
**l** written  **m** chosen  **n** put  **o** ridden  **p** agreed
**q** travelled  **r** driven  **s** tried

**2**  **a** Have; been  **b** hasn't; seen  **c** Have; studied
**d** have; flown  **e** have; visited  **f** Has; had

**3**  **a** Have you ever tried Indian food? No, I haven't.
**b** Have you ever studied English before? Yes, I have.
**c** Has he ever sent an e-mail before? No, he hasn't.
**d** Has she ever driven in Britain? Yes, she has.
**e** Has she ever ridden a camel? Yes, she has.
**f** Has he ever spoken to you before? No, he hasn't.

**4**  **a** has she lived in London?
**b** How long has she taught at the university?
**c** How long has she had a cat?
**d** has he been a student?
**e** How long has he studied music?
**f** How long has he played the piano?

## Unit 6

**A**  1–c; 2–d; 3–a; 4–b

**1**  **a** hasn't picked; yet  **b** has already done
**c** has just washed  **d** has already peeled
**e** hasn't cooked; yet  **f** has already made
**g** hasn't done; yet

**2**  b–4; c–2; d–1; e–6; f–3; g–5

**3**  **a** has moved  **b** has changed  **c** has got
**d** has saved  **e** has bought  **f** has grown
**g** has started

## Unit 7

**A**  **2** past simple  **3** past simple  **4** past simple
**5** present perfect  **6** present perfect

**1**  Past simple: last Tuesday, What time?, yesterday, ago,
last week
Present perfect: this week, yet, just, since, already, ever

**2**  **1** Have visited; went  **2** did; start/begin;
started/ began  **3** has lost  **4** has prepared; has
washed up  **5** Did; see; did  **6** has had
**7** Have; done; did; went

**3**  **a** went  **b** was  **c** visited  **d** had  **e** has been
**f** since  **g** came  **h** ago  **i** only arrived
**j** has already phoned  **k** hasn't unpacked
**l** hasn't done  **m** yet

**4**  **a** How long did he stay in Pakistan? He stayed there
three weeks.
**b** What did he do in Pakistan? He visited all his
relatives.
**c** How many times has he been to Pakistan? He's been
there three times.
**d** When did he come to live in England? He came here
two years ago.
**e** When did he arrive back? He arrived back last
weekend.
**f** What has he done since he came back? He's phoned
Rafiq.
**g** What hasn't he done yet? He hasn't unpacked and
done all his washing.

## Unit 8

**A**  **1** If; open; get  **2** If; go; can ask
**3** Take; if; want  **4** If; go; I'll come
**5** I'll let; when; go

**B**  **2** T  **3** T  **4** F  **5** T

**C**  1

**1**  **a** ~~'ll see~~ see  **b** ~~'ll be~~ are  **c** ~~won't~~ doesn't  **d** ~~Do~~ Will
**e** ~~won't~~ don't  **f** ~~doesn't~~ won't

**2**  b–1; c–2; d–5; e–4; f–3

**3**  **a** when  **b** When  **c** if  **d** when  **e** When  **f** if

**4**  **1 a** lose; eat  **b** is; need  **c** join; meet
**2 a** snows; will build  **b** will be; learn
**c** won't get; don't look

## Unit 9.1

**A**  **1** are; m  **2** Are; s  **3** weren't; was
**4** have been; ve been  **5** Will; be; 'll be

**1**  **a** are  **b** have been  **c** weren't  **d** will be
**e** Were you  **f** hasn't been  **g** will be  **h** 'm not

**2** **a** ~~has~~ is   **b** ~~doesn't be~~ isn't   **c** ~~was~~ were
**d** ~~'m will~~ will be   **e** ~~There~~ It
**f** ~~Did you was~~ Were you
**g** ~~have~~ has   **h** ~~has~~ is

**3** **a** will be/is   **b** were   **c** was   **d** isn't/is   **e** will be
**f** have been   **g** Will; be   **h** hasn't been

## Unit 9.2

**A** **1** ve got   **2** Do; have   **3** Did; have   **4** didn't
**5** have; had   **6** haven't   **7** ll have

**1** **a** ~~has got~~ has   **b** ~~had~~ did   **c** ~~hadn't~~ haven't
**d** ~~had have~~ have got   **e** ~~had~~ had
**f** ~~had not~~ didn't have   **g** ~~get~~ got   **h** ~~Did~~ Have

**2** **a** Have; got/Do; have; haven't/don't
**b** haven't had   **c** Did; have; did   **d** have
**e** Have; got/Do; have; haven't/don't
**f** haven't got/don't have   **g** Have; had; have
**h** ll have

## Unit 10

**A** **2** does the course cost   **3** I need to go
**b** when the lessons start   **a** how much the course
costs   **c** where I need to go

**B** **1** a class on Wednesday afternoons
**2** Do I need to buy any books

**1** **a** Do you know where she lives?
**b** Can you tell me which platform the train leaves
from?
**c** I'd like to know how much this sweater costs.
**d** Have you any idea where the paper is?
**e** Please could you tell me how I get to the bus station?
**f** Have you decided what you are going to wear
tonight?

**2** **a** ~~does cost a return ticket~~ a return ticket costs
**b** ~~did the teacher give~~ the teacher gave
**c** ~~from where does come the new student~~ where the
new student comes from
**d** ~~on which street does she live~~ which street she lives on
**e** ~~have you~~ you have   **f** ~~to where are you going~~ where
you are going to

**3** Example answers:
**a** Do you know why the photocopier isn't working?
**b** Can you tell me how much milk you like in your
coffee?
**c** Could you tell me where the nearest toilet is?
**d** Do you know how much it costs by taxi?
**e** Can you tell me what you are going to eat?
**f** Do you know what the time is?
**g** Could you tell me how this machine works?

**4** **a** 3   **b** 2   **c** 3

**5** **a** you like fish?   **b** if/whether anyone phoned me
yesterday?   **c** you tell me if/whether you are from
Pakistan?   **d** you know if the post has come?
**e** Could you tell me if/whether the sports centre is
open on Sunday evenings?
**f** Do you know/Can you tell me if/whether I have to
wear a suit?

## Unit 11.1

**A** **1** tell   **2** say

**1** **a** said   **b** tell   **c** said   **d** tells   **e** said   **f** tell   **g** say
**h** telling   **i** said

**2** **a** he; her   **b** they   **c** me; I; my   **d** you; him

**3** **a** Rafiq said that he doesn't like hamburgers.
**b** The teacher told the student that the lesson is in the
computer room.
**c** My father told me about my grandfather's life.
**d** You must tell me if you are worried.
**e** He told me he is leaving at 8 o'clock.
**f** She said she thinks her teacher is very nice.
**g** Deva didn't say there is a problem.

## Unit 11.2

**A** had, would, could, liked

**1** **a** had   **b** was going   **c** couldn't   **d** went   **e** would
**f** didn't want   **g** wouldn't   **h** liked

**2** **a** he would   **b** she had   **c** he was   **d** they had
**e** she didn't   **f** he wouldn't
**g** she didn't think she would

**3** **a** he went to college two evenings a week
**b** he couldn't write English very well
**c** me he liked his teachers
**d** he had studied English for three months
**e** me he didn't like using computers
**f** he was going to university next year
**g** me he hadn't taken any English exams

## Unit 12.1

**A** Type 1: when you would be home
Type 2: if you could phone him back

**1** **a** how long; if   **b** if; where   **c** if; how
**d** what time; if   **e** what; if

**2** **a** if I had any children.
**b** her if she was doing anything on Saturday.
**c** when I had arrived in this country.
**d** me if I could work late.
**e** her friend what time she got up on Sundays.
**f** me if I had ever visited Poland.   **g** if I knew her sister.

**3** **a** if I could spell my name/to spell my name
**b** if I was married
**c** if she could see my passport
**d** how long I was going to stay here
**e** when I would leave the college
**f** if/whether I had studied English before
**g** if/whether I had (got) a visa

## Unit 12.2

**A** Type 1: my phone number   Type 2: to fill in a form

**1** **a** ✓   **b** ~~to~~ for   **c** ✓   **d** ~~for~~   **e** asked me for   **f** ✓
**g** ~~for helping~~ to help

**2** b–5; c–2; d–1; e–7; f–8; g–4; h–3

**3** **a** to open the window  **b** know the time
**c** to phone the doctor  **d** to get some shopping
for her  **e** for a pencil  **f** not to tell anyone her secret
**g** age

## Unit 13

**A** to swim; to get; putting; swimming; swim; to swim;
swimming; do; to go; to get; to get; drive

**B** 2 to get  3 swim

**C** Verbs + -ing: don't mind; go
Prepositions: at
Verbs + to -: learn; want; would like; hope
Adjectives + to -: easy; difficult
Modal verbs: can; should; would; will

**1** **a** before  **b** expect  **c** important  **d** expensive
**e** could  **f** must

**2** like, start, love, hate

**3** **a** to have  **b** shopping  **c** buy  **d** meeting
**e** to buy  **f** preparing  **g** working  **h** to help
**i** to rent  **j** phone  **k** to give  **l** smoking
**m** playing

## Unit 14.1

**A** 2 living  3 driving  4 understanding

**1** **a** Writing in English is difficult for me.
**b** Smoking can be bad for your health.
**c** Working at night makes me tired.
**d** Drinking water is very good for you.
**e** Flying is faster than travelling by train.
**f** Studying at college is interesting and good fun.
**g** Switching off your mobile phone is necessary in the
cinema.

**2** **a** Going swimming  **b** Drinking a lot of water
**c** Speaking English  **d** Using the computer a lot
makes  **e** Riding a bike is a cheap form of
**f** Listening to music is my favourite hobby.
**g** Getting up late on Sundays is possible for me.

## Unit 14.2

**A** 1 to improve  2 to learn; to get

**1** **a** ✓  **b** for  **c** getting to get  **d** ✓  **e** for to  **f** ✓
**g** ✓  **h** For

**2** **a** to have  **b** to see about  **c** to lose  **d** to make
**e** to become  **f** to get  **g** to tell  **h** to call  **i** to meet

## Unit 15.1

**A** 2 must  3 need to  4 Do; have to  5 had to
**6** don't have to  7 mustn't

**1** **a** had to  **b** mustn't  **c** have to  **d** have to
**e** don't have to  **f** didn't have to  **g** need to

**2** **a** to  **b** have  **c** had  **d** mustn't  **e** to  **f** had
**g** Did  **h** don't  **i** have/need

## Unit 15.2

**A** 2 ought to go  3 Should I register  4 you could
phone  5 I would  6 would be  7 must take

**1** b–8; c–4; d–7; e–2; f–5; g–3; h–1

**2** Must Could/Can; would can/could/'ll; ought I to
do/should I do; you would I would

## Unit 16.1

**A** 2 I'll definitely  3 I'll certainly  4 I think I'll
**5** I'll probably  6 I might  7 I could  8 I may

**1** **a** ✓  **b** won't definitely definitely won't  **c** ✓  **d**
won't probably probably won't  **e** ✓  **f** want won't

**2** **a** 'll definitely/certainly finish
**b** may/might/could see him
**c** may/might/could rain
**d** probably/almost certainly won't take
**e** might/may/could be  **f** may/might/could buy
**g** definitely/certainly won't pass

## Unit 16.2

**A** 2 May I  3 Could I  4 Can I  5 Can you
**6** Could you

**1** **a** to help  **b** ✓  **c** may could/can  **d** ✓
**e** mind you Do you mind  **f** can I I can  **g** ✓

**2** **a** May I borrow your pen, please?
**b** Can you help me with this letter, please?
**c** Could I give you the report tomorrow?
**d** Could you tell me what the time is, please?
**e** Do you mind if I ask you why you came to this
country?

**3** Example answers:
**a** Excuse me, but may we see the menu, please?
**b** Excuse me, could we have a look at the wine list,
please?
**c** Can you bring some iced water, please?
**d** Sorry, but could I change my knife and fork?
**e** Excuse me, could you close the window, please?
**f** Sorry, but may I use the phone, please?
**g** Excuse me, could you tell me where the toilets are?

## Unit 17.1

**A** 2 that  3 whose

**B** 1 who  2 that  3 whose

**1** **a** which  **b** who  **c** that  **d** whose  **e** that  **f** who
**g** who

**2** **a** which it is  **b** whose who  **c** that's whose
**d** which it is  **e** who which/that  **f** that she who
**g** that whose

**3**    **a** I looked at the clock on the wall which/that was broken.
**b** This is the friend of mine whose daughter got married last Saturday.
**c** My boss is the manager who/that is responsible for the company's finances.
**d** They are building some new houses which/that are very expensive.
**e** We met a writer at the party whose books are very famous.
**f** I spoke to someone on the phone who/that told me I had the wrong number.
**g** Dogs are animals which/that can be very intelligent.

## Unit 17.2

**A**    This is the pool where we sunbathed all day.

**1**    **a** There are lots of mountains in the country where I live.
**b** She put her jewellery in a secret place where nobody could find it.
**c** That's the restaurant where they serve really good fish.
**d** The office where I work is in the city centre.
**e** The pub where we went was very noisy.
**f** The market where I get my vegetables comes to town every Saturday.
**g** The airport where the plane landed was very small.

**2**    **a** This is the bus that/which
**b** This is the airport where    **c** This is the man who
**d** This is the barman who    **e** This is the woman who
**f** This is the market which/that
**g** This is the beach where

## Unit 18.1

**A**    **3** Yes    **4** No

**1**    Not necessary: a, c, f, g

**2**    **b** they thought was acting strangely.
**c** which/that is broken.
**d** I keep all my information in.
**e** who live next door to you?
**f** I've had so much trouble with.
**g** which/that is just around the corner.
**h** the company has just employed.

## Unit 18.2

**A**    a barbecue on

**1**    **a** ✓    **b** where    **c** ✓    **d** what    **e** at to    **f** in    **g** ✓

**2**    **a** 1 I lived    2 I lived in    **b** 1 I work    2 I work for
**c** 1 she lives    2 the street she lives on
**d** 1 I wait    2 the bus stop I wait at    **e** 1 I study
2 I study at is very old    **f** 1 he goes is in the city centre
2 he goes to is in the city centre    **g** 1 The supermarket where I do my shopping is open 24 hours    2 The supermarket I do my shopping at is open 24 hours

## Unit 19

**A**    **a** as    **b** Although    **c** because    **d** and also    **e** and
**f** Also    **g** so    **h** or

**1**    **a** because    **b** so    **c** and    **d** or    **e** although    **f** Also
**g** so

**2**    **a** so    **b** but    **c** or    **d** although    **e** because    **f** also

**3**    **a** although because/as    **b** but and also    **c** or and
**d** because so    **e** So Although    **f** as but/although
**g** so as/because

**4**    **a** so    **b** and    **c** as/because    **d** Also    **e** and    **f** So
**g** but    **h** and    **i** although    **j** so

## Unit 20

**A**    **1** No    **2** Yes    **3** Yes    **4** No    **5** No    **6** No    **7** Yes

**B**    **1** in hospital    **2** at work; home    **3** lunch; dinner
**4** university; medicine    **5** television; the radio; the cinema    **6** next; last

**C**    **1** the rice; the vegetables    **2** the alcohol    **3** the food
**4** the food; the fat; the salt; the sugar    **5** The children

**1**    the following need *the*: b, d, e, h, j, k, n

**2**    **a** ✓    **b** the Alps; the next week    **c** ✓    **d** the classical music    **e** the prison; the murder    **f** ✓
**g** the last night; the cinema    **h** ✓

## Unit 21

**A**    busiest; more exciting; better; smaller; more peaceful, the furthest; livelier; the most beautiful; the worst; more; less

**B**    more peaceful; more exciting; livelier; better; the biggest; the most beautiful; busiest; the worst; the furthest/farthest

**1**    **a** nearer; the nearest    **b** happier; the happiest
**c** farther/further; the farthest/furthest
**d** more interesting; the most interesting
**e** more careful; the most careful    **f** more expensive, the most expensive    **g** worse; the worst    **h** sadder; the saddest    **i** slimmer; the slimmest    **j** friendlier; the friendliest    **k** safer; the safest

**2**    **a** prettyest prettiest    **b** weter wetter    **c** longer longest    **d** than that    **e** worst worse    **f** more moderner    **g** the latest    **h** more friendlier

**3**    **a** slower and older than; faster and younger than
**b** busier and more exciting than; calmer and more peaceful than

**4**    Example answers:
**a** 2 the busiest, oldest, biggest    3 the most attractive, most romantic    **b** 1 the most difficult and most rewarding    2 the most interesting and best-paid
3 has the worst, least interesting and dirtiest

## Unit 22.1

**A** as as; not as; as; a lot more interesting; a bit later, far less dirty, much better paid

**1** **a** a bit better paid than  **b** as tall as
**c** much less clean  **d** a lot more beautiful than
**e** n't as interesting as  **f** far younger than
**g** as comfortable as

**2** **a** than  **b** lot  **c** much  **d** as  **e** bit/little  **f** more
**g** later

**3** Example answers: **a** modern as  **b** larger than
**c** interesting as house 3  **d** noisier than house 3
**e** as peaceful as house 3  **f** a bit cheaper than house 2
**g** a lot more expensive than the other two/house 1 and house 2

## Unit 22.2

**A** **2** a  **3** b  **4** b

**1** **a** He isn't old enough to leave school.
**b** She is beautiful enough to be a model.
**c** The car is a bit too expensive for me to buy.
**d** The skirt was too short for her to wear to work.
**e** The lessons aren't long enough for us to practise our English.

**2** **a** too late to do the exam.
**b** too tired to go to the party.
**c** cheap enough (for us) to buy.
**d** too heavy (for me) to carry.  **e** clear enough to read.
**f** well enough to go to school.
**g** experienced enough to get the job.

## Unit 23

**A** Questions and negatives: any; Affirmatives: some

**B** Uncountable: a little; much; a little; Countable: many; a few; many; a few

**C** Most; Some; Most of the; Some of them

**1** **a** some  **b** much  **c** a little  **d** any  **e** a lot of
**f** many; many; a few  **g** a lot of

**2** **a** any/many/a lot of  **b** a little/some/a lot of
**c** a few/some  **d** some/a little; much/a lot
**e** any/much/a lot of  **f** some/a lot of
**g** any/many/a lot of; many/a lot; a few

**3** **a** All of cities  **b** Some of my  **c** ✓  **d** ✓
**e** all of them  **f** ✓

**4** Use *of* in: a, c, f, g

## Unit 24

**A** on; at

**B** **2** from; till  **3** for  **4** while; during

**1** **a** in at  **b** on at  **c** in the at  **d** on in  **e** at in
**f** in at  **g** in on

**2** **a** at  **b** in  **c** on  **d** in  **e** in  **f** at  **g** on  **h** in
**i** in  **j** in  **k** at  **l** on  **m** at  **n** on  **o** at  **p** at
**q** in  **r** on  **s** on  **t** in  **u** at  **v** in  **w** in

**3** **a** during  **b** for  **c** during  **d** by  **e** for
**f** from; till  **g** while  **h** for  **i** during  **j** from; till
**k** while  **l** by/from  **m** by

**4** **a** during while  **b** for from; by till  **c** during while
**d** till by  **e** while during  **f** during for  **g** by while

## Unit 25.1

**A** **1** at  **2** to  **3** of  **4** on  **5** in  **6** on  **7** to
**8** in  **9** with

**1** **a** on  **b** in  **c** to  **d** from  **e** with  **f** about  **g** to
**h** of  **i** in  **j** in  **k** of

**2** b–8; c–6; d–1; e–4; f–7; g–3; h–5

**3** **a** of  **b** at  **c** for  **d** with  **e** about  **f** at  **g** in
**h** about  **i** for

## Unit 25.2

**A** **1** in  **2** to  **3** by  **4** on  **5** in; of

**1** **a** by  **b** on  **c** in  **d** on  **e** In  **f** at  **g** in  **h** on
**i** in  **j** home  **k** at

**2** **a** on  **b** in  **c** by  **d** with  **e** in  **f** in  **g** on
**h** on  **i** on  **j** into/out of  **k** in

## Unit 26

**A** **1** look; up  **2** looking after  **3** looking forward to

**B** **1** look forward to  **2** look out  **3** look up

**C** Type 2: up; up; up  Type 3: after; forward to

**1** **a** after  **b** in  **c** on  **d** on  **e** out  **f** back  **g** in

**2** **a** up  **b** up  **c** off  **d** up  **e** down  **f** away
**g** in; down

**3** **a** switch  **b** put  **c** take  **d** put  **e** knock  **f** get
**g** work

**4** **a** Take off them Take them off; put your slippers on ✓
**b** I drop my kids off ✓ pick them up ✓
**c** washed the dishes up ✓ ; dry up them dry them up
**d** I put the phone down ✓ ; cut off me cut me off
**e** tidy up my room ✓ ; throw all the rubbish away ✓
**f** running petrol out of running out of petrol; fill the car up ✓
**g** I gave up smoking ✓ ; I took up it took it up

**Published by**
Garnet Publishing Ltd.
8 Southern Court
South Street
Reading RG1 4QS, UK

www.garneteducation.com

This edition first published 2007.

ISBN 978 1 85964 897 1

British Library Cataloguing-in-Publication Data
A catalogue record for this book is available from
the British Library.

**Acknowledgements**
I am grateful for the help of Fiona McGarry in reading and
commenting on the manuscript. I would also like to thank
Sue Messenger, and the students and teachers in the Skills
for Life Department at Central Sussex College.

The writing of this book necessarily involves reference to
the corpus of published grammar reference books. In this
respect, I would like to acknowledge in particular the work
of M Swan & C Walter (OUP), R Murphy (CUP) and
D Beaumont & C Granger (Macmillan/Heinemann).

**Production**
Project manager:       Fiona McGarry
Project consultant:    Rod Webb
Editorial team:        Richard Peacock, Emily Clarke,
                       Francesca Pinagli, Martin Moore
Design:                Robert Jones
Layout:                Carole White, Nick Asher
Illustration:          Doug Nash
Photography:           Clipart.com, Corbis, Getty Images

Every effort has been made to trace the copyright holders
and we apologize in advance for any unintentional
omissions. We will be happy to insert the appropriate
acknowledgements in any subsequent editions.

**Printed and bound**
in Lebanon by International Press